Treat People Like Dogs!

Six tasks for passionate leaders

Other books by Author

Robert Norton. *Communicator style: Theory, applications, and measures.* 1983, Sage Publications.

Robert Norton and David Brenders. *Communication and consequences: Laws of interaction.* 1997, Erlbaum Publications.

Treat People Like Dogs!

Six tasks for **passionate leaders**

Robert Norton

Wild Norton Fire
P.O. Box 4793
Butte, Montana 59701
www.wildnortonfire.com

Produced by **Wild Norton Fire** in the United States.

Copyright © Robert Norton 2005.

Front cover: Frank Turner and Mischief.

Norton, Robert, 2005. *Treat people like dogs! Six tasks for passionate leaders.*

ISBN 1-876555416

1. Leadership. 2. High performance teams. 3. Dogs. I. Title.

Digital production by Friesens. Printed in Canada by Friesens, Altona, Manitoba, Canada ROG 080.

To the mushers and the people who support them.
And, to all individuals who dare to embrace a worthy
quest, bring life to their values, get the right people in
the right jobs, obtain permission to lead, develop an
iron will, and contribute to the community.

Contents

Call of the wild and other stirrings

For my birthday, my wife and I take a month off to ride our motorbikes from Montana to Alaska and back, 4000+ miles, the distance to the center of the earth. Catherine wants to visit a guy called Frank Turner when we get to Whitehorse in the Yukon.

He gives educational talks daily about dog sledding. I press her to see why she wants to do this. She says that she uses the example of the dog team in her leadership workshops. She contrasts the musher as a leader from behind to someone like Winston Churchill, a leader from the front.

Muktuk Kennels

We drive to Muktuk Kennels nestled in the hills on the bank of the Takhini River 14 miles from Whitehorse. When we get there, we see a small group of people gathered around a short man.

He has a bushy brown and gray beard, rimless glasses, tufts of

1

gray hair sticking out of his baseball cap, and a mischievous, lopsided grin.

Frank Turner, Veteran Yukon Quest musher, runs Muktuk Kennels in the Yukon.

We see over 100 dogs next to their doghouses, like a little city, ten in every row. Each dog's chain is long enough that it can visit its closest neighbors.

The dogs bark continually. We shout an introduction to Frank. When he begins the talk he yells, *"Quiiii-et!"* Every dog shuts up—silence in a second. Amazing. He wins me right then and there.

Frank tells his story. He has entered the Yukon Quest 22 times. It is a 1000-mile dog sled race up the Yukon River which is frozen in the winter. Fourteen dogs, one sled, and one driver make up the team. The musher carries all that is needed for survival.

The Quest rules are stringent. The mushers must use only the sled they start with. They cannot accept any help except at the half way mark. The Quest website describes the race:

2

The race route runs on frozen rivers, climbs four mountain ranges, and passes through isolated, northern villages. With temperatures hitting "40 below", "100 mile-an-hour" winds, open water and bad ice all working against the teams, the Yukon Quest is a true test of the capacity of humans and canines, and a tribute to the strength of the ancient bond that unites them.

The team of 14 dogs takes 81,000,000 steps to get to the finish line. They average about 8 to 10 miles per hour. Frank talks about how he needs a team, not a group of 14 dogs.

A team is a very special group of individuals. He knows after a certain amount of training that the moment will come when he "has a team." Every dog pulls one hundred percent in sync. He feels it even with his eyes closed.

Catherine is in bliss, nodding agreement like mad. When we walk to the river, he releases a dozen dogs. We have dog biscuits to feed them. He instructs us how to feed them. *Put it firmly in front of their mouths. Look them in the eyes and note the different personalities.* Each dog takes the treat differently, never biting.

The eyes vary. Some are steely blue, others chocolate brown, and others almost white. They knit their brows, and pull their lips back as though smiling, or even leering.

The dogs race up and down the trail past us in packs. They play their own game. They charge at us and then dodge at the last second. All the time, Frank tells his story. We go back to the two-story log house to see a video of last year's Quest. Frank is in it.

We see the toil, danger, and beauty of 1000 miles of isolation, cold, and dark.

After a snack of tea and homemade muffins we go to his basement where he shows his sled and describes his procedures. Three hours extend to four and he goes on.

Return to Muktuk

I return two months later and stay with Frank and his family at Muktuk Kennels. I tell him that I would like to write a book about him and his dogs, but initially I do not want to share with him the perspective. I do not want answers he thinks I might want to hear.

When it is written, I will share everything. He can change or comment on anything. At that point, we can have a good conversation about the perspective. He smiles and warns me that he has never read a book about the Yukon Quest and finds it almost impossible to read anything written about him. Nevertheless, he welcomes me to Muktuk.

Frank naturally inspires although he does not consciously think about it. He doesn't talk about leadership principles. He's a musher, a person who drives a team of dogs pulling a dogsled.

However, what he does with a dog team and, more importantly, what he does in his community haunts and taunts me to examine my own work.

At the least interesting end of the continuum, I deliver programs to companies that need to tick a box or want the consulting trick de jour. I use all kinds of instruments to measure things from the worthless to the critical. I sheep dip employees through programs of improvement, build teams, and enhance customer service. I facilitate workshops that range from company diversions to strategic planning.

At the most interesting end of the continuum, I put out fires or create them, namely working with companies suffering catastrophic crisis, chronic underperformance, or creeping mediocrity. Frank's example challenges me.

I know people aren't dogs, but metaphorical connections flood my thinking. The northern wilderness puts me in a reflective state. Jack London hovers closely.

At first, I think Frank's story is simple. He is a long time musher who trains dogs like any other animal trainer. He makes it work by persistence.

But the simple story becomes a riddle. Frank is a passionate leader. It seems obvious that **if every person or organization treated people like dogs, the way Frank treats his dogs, they would prosper.**

Bigger questions nag at me. Essentially, this book unravels an example of a beautiful operation that fosters and depends upon high performance teams, not only among Alaskan Huskies, arguably the most exceptional athletes in the world, but also among a staff of apprentices from around the world. The work profoundly influences the community, family, and Frank.

An aside

When my son, Rob, graduates from high school, I encourage him to apply to Muktuk Kennels to work with Frank. Subsequently, he spends six weeks in the Yukon where he becomes an expert at the "poop scoop," learns what dogs eat and how to feed and water them, and how to harness dogs for training runs.

Frank and Anne graciously allow him to go with them for parts of the 2005 Yukon Quest. He gains unimagined experience, sees the northern lights, and knows over 100 dogs. He experiences Frank and his community, and sees a passionate leader in action who knows how to treat people and dogs.

Your invitation

I invite you to take a journey with me in this book. In each chapter **make connections to your life**, relationships and work.

Throughout the book I nod to Jack London who follows the 1897 gold rush into the Yukon when he is 20. He carouses with an outrageously colorful cast of characters, absorbs their stories, hears the call of the wild, and discovers more of himself.

Before he dies at the age of 40, he writes 51 books including *The call of the wild* and *White Fang*. He is one of America's foremost authors.

The call of the wild is also your call. You know what it is deep down. But you don't need to be in the Yukon. The wild calls you right now where you are. Extraordinary people, stories of hope and courage, and the wonderment of self-discovery wait for you. They will trigger something in you.

The extended metaphor of treating people like dogs is a version of the golden rule. It is the foundation of your journey in this book where you encounter six life tasks that every passionate leader should pursue:

1. Get a worthy quest!
2. Bring life to your values!
3. Get the right people in the right jobs!
4. Obtain permission to lead!
5. Develop an iron will!
6. Foster community support!

They are tasks because they require attentive effort to move toward objectives. They are life tasks because they encourage you to live with energy and learn obsessively each day.

The tasks are for individuals who want to lead not because they covet power, but because they passionately believe. The passion means they live their values so saliently, so intensely, that they want to share it with friends, family, and associates.

Let's explore the call of the wild. **Let's find out what it means to treat people like dogs.**

chapter one

Get a worthy quest!

As the individual searches for meaning, something unexpected happens. **The search itself becomes meaningful.**

A worthy quest gives individuals more than they bargain for. It changes them. Jason and the Argonauts, Meriwether Lewis and William Clark, Don Quixote and Sancho, and Alexander the Great find themselves in journeys so transforming that the concept of failure makes little sense.

Being "in" the journey of a worthy quest, no matter how harsh or difficult, rewards the person. The individual witnesses a process that allows both primal discoveries and complex learning. The quest kindles desire, sparks interest, and fires creativity. The person intensely lives in the "now" and at the same time anticipates the forces of the future.

Passionate leaders know the power of a worthy quest.

Northern quests

In the late 1800s, gold fever drives thousands of individuals to passionately pursue quests that change their lives forever.

The explorers snake their way north after the 1848 California gold rush. Tens of thousands dream, dare, and accept northern quests. The gold rush promises instant wealth, but delivers a lifetime of experience that money can't buy.

Prospectors lead the frenzy. In 1857, the Frasier River valley in southern British Columbia yields placer gold (already free from the rock). The miner doesn't need fancy equipment.

Simultaneously, fur traders and trappers travel through the territory from as far away as the Aleutian Islands to the Mackenzie and Porcupine Rivers in the Northwest Territories of Canada. Rumors of gold follow their paths.

In 1871, the rugged interior Caribou Mountains further north yield gold (3 million ounces eventually) followed in 1874 by the discovery of gold fields in British Columbia's Cassiar Mountains near the Yukon border.

The Stickeen River takes the miners further north along the Alaskan Coast. In 1880, Silver Bow Basin, now Juneau, gives up gold.

In 1885, reports of gold, ranging in size from fine grains like corn meal to larger grains like wheat kernels, send over 200 miners to the Stewart River in the Yukon and then to Forty-Mile, then Sixty-Mile in 1893 and Birch Creek in 1894.

After luring many charac-ters to the territory for the inevitable big discovery, the fickle Muses smile on an unlikely trio of men: George W. Carmack, a white man, married to an Indian woman, and two Tagish Indians, Skookum Jim and Cultus (nicknamed "Worth-less") Charlie. Carmack pre-fers to live with the Indians.

Carmack, Charley, and Skookum Jim start the biggest gold rush in history.

In August 1896, lightning finally strikes at Rabbit Creek, a branch of the Klondike River. When Carmack files the claims at Forty-Mile, the town empties. The locals stake claims up and down the creek.

Even then, dog sled races occur. When a claim near Skookum Jim's opens, a mounted policeman announces at midnight that anybody can stake it. Lereaux and Vaughan stake it and race for Dawson with a six dog sled team. Lowerie and an Indian com-panion follow closely with the same number of dogs. They reach the recorder's office at the same time and split the claim.

Excelsior docks July 16, 1897, at San Francisco. It brings the first news of the Yukon gold rush. The Portland docks one day later in Seattle with $700,000 in gold.

Stampede to Yukon

It takes over a year for the news to reach the outside world. In July 1897, the *Seattle Post-Intelligencer* proclaims the sensational news after the Portland docks in Seattle:

GOLD! GOLD! GOLD! GOLD!

Sixty-Eight Rich Men on the Steamer Portland.

STACKS OF YELLOW METAL!

Some Have $5000. Many Have More, and a Few Bring Out $100,000 Each.

THE STEAMER CARRIES $700,000.

12

The news flames the imagination of the world. One out of seven of Seattle's 67,000 citizens head to the Yukon:

> Outfitters were sending frantic telegrams for more supplies. Farms were mortgaged, pools were formed and straws drawn to see who would take the grubstake and run for the Klondike. Policemen, firemen, streetcar conductors, newspaper reporters, and others quit their jobs on the spur of the moment and headed north. (Archie Satterfield, *Chilkoot Pass*)

A majority of the gold seekers takes a steamer to Skagway, Alaska, and go to Dyea, a small township at the end of Lynn Canal. From here they hike 26 miles. Chilkoot Pass is the major obstacle.

Once over the pass, they hike to Lake Lindeman and then to Lake Bennett, and then get on the Yukon River for 550 miles to Dawson City where the Klondike River begins. At that junction, the stampeder heads up the Klondike River toward the gold fields.

If they had known at the beginning of the journey that others had claimed and worked the gold fields for almost two years, they might have turned back. They do not imagine they will end up working for the old timers. The hope of striking it rich still drives them.

At Chilkoot Pass the stampeders climb 1200 steps, called the Golden Stairs, chipped out of snow and ice on a 30-degee slope for a total vertical climb of 500 feet.

An endless string of people climb the Golden Stairs at Chilkoot Pass. Note the individuals sliding back down the pass.

The Canadian government requires that each outsider brings 2000 pounds of provisions to survive a year in the Yukon. They must bring food (flour, bacon, split peas and beans top the list), tools (pick, shovel, gold pan, axe, and saws), cooking gear (fry pan, pie plate, knife and fork, cup) and other things like nails, compass, tent, boots, and clothes.

The stampeder carries 60 to 70 pounds each trek. An unbroken, single file line of climbers stretches to the summit. If anyone gets

VIEW SHOWING THE MODE OF TRAVEL ON THE CHILKOOT.

Once climbers reached the top, this is the view they saw before sliding down.

off the trail for any reason, it takes hours to get back in line.

After an hour's climb the person plunges back down the mountain, sliding on a shovel or anything else that is handy. It takes 30 or more trips to get the mandatory ton of goods to the top of the pass.

To complete the summit leg, each person accumulatively climbs 36,000 steps, travels six miles, and ascends 15,000 vertical feet, higher than any of Canada's coastal mountains.

The next leg requires the stampeder to relay the ton of goods to Crater Lake, and then by sled or horses to either Lake Lindeman or Lake Bennett. The relays balloon the trek from Skagway to Lake Bennett into almost 2000 miles for some.

Blizzards rage. Winds cut to the quick. The temperature drops to a numbing -50° F. Up to 70 feet of snow falls. On April 3, 1898, an avalanche kills 63 people.

Both trails end at Lake Bennett leaving 550 miles to run the rapids down the Yukon River. But, they cannot go until the lake thaws. Tens of thousands camp on Lake Bennett's shores. They scavenge wood to build something they have never built—boats.

On May 28, 1898, the ice begins to break up and by the 29th, a circus of 7000 boats starts down the lake. Unbelievable.

They go from Lake Bennett to Whitehorse to Lake Laberge to Hootalinqua to Five Fingers Rapids to Rink Rapids to Fort Selkirk to Steward to Dawson City. In a two-year period, 30,000 people climb the trail.

And, today, that is essentially the first half of the trail that the Yukon Quest dogsled race honors. The second half follows the gold rush from Dawson City to Fairbanks, Alaska.

Yukon Quest

The Yukon Quest dogsled race celebrates all the people, young and old, romantics and realists, who make the northern quests. It honors the trappers, gold seekers, traders, and mail carriers who travel north. It remembers when traders and dog teams are the lifelines to the frozen, isolated communities especially in the winter, when eight to ten dogs in single file pull large freight sleds to equip the miners.

Mail is as valuable as food. Any news is good news even if it is old news. If you are a passenger on one of these sleds, you run along side it to keep it lighter for the dogs. You ride only when you need a rest. The trails are dangerous. In 1901, a dog team and mail carrier crash through the ice and die.

The Quest commemorates the settlers who stay to form tiny communities up and down the trail from Whitehorse, Yukon to Fairbanks, Alaska. Every year they rotate the starting point.

Route

The race challenges the mushers to drive their dog team 1000 miles in the coldest part of the winter through a variety of terrain over four mountains. The first part of the race takes the mushers from Whitehorse to Dawson. They travel about 500 miles north and northwest. All rookies attend mandatory meetings to clarify the exact route of the race and to offer the best advice to do well. Experienced mushers share their knowledge.

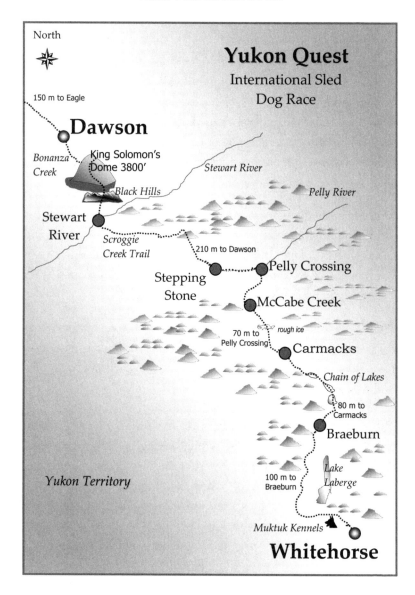

North

Yukon Quest
International Sled
Dog Race

150 m to Eagle

Dawson

*Bonanza
Creek*

King Solomon's
Dome 3800'

Stewart River

Black Hills

Pelly River

Stewart
River

*Scroggie
Creek Trail*

210 m to Dawson

Stepping
Stone

Pelly Crossing

McCabe Creek

70 m to
Pelly Crossing

rough ice

Carmacks

Chain of Lakes

80 m to
Carmacks

Braeburn

Yukon Territory

100 m to
Braeburn

*Lake
Laberge*

Muktuk Kennels

Whitehorse

They begin at Whitehorse, elevation 2305 ft. They climb to Brae-burn (2400 ft), drop down to Carmacks (1770 ft), then begin the climb to Pelly Crossing (1870 ft), then up the first mountain to King Solomon's Dome (3800 ft).

At this point, Dawson City is not far where they can accept help during the mandatory, 36-hour stop. Mushers and dogs rest. After Dawson, they head for the Alaska-Yukon border.

When they leave Dawson City, they climb to American Summit (3420 ft), and then drop to Eagle (880 ft) and Circle City (610 ft).

From here, they climb back up to Central (932 ft) and Eagle Summit (3650 ft). They drop to Mile 101 (2398 ft) and climb the last mountain, Rosebud (3480 ft). Then, Angel Creek (1000 ft), North Pole (483 ft), and, finally, Fairbanks (434 ft) completes the last leg.

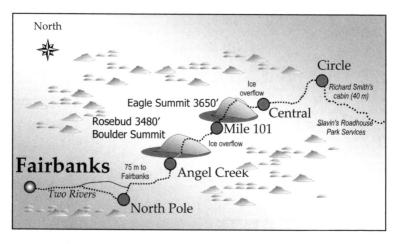

The median time across all Quests is about 11.3 days. There are ten checkpoints along the route, some more than 200 miles apart. They will climb 8448 vertical feet over the course. It is the toughest dogsled race in the world.

Rules

The mushers must be self-sufficient enough to aid any other

musher in real need of help. The individual must survive in profound cold, unforgiving storms, ripping wind, mountains, dangerous water and ice, and isolation.

Only a musher can assist another musher. Even in the heat of the competition, the code of the trail calls for providing assistance. **A win without honor is hollow.**

The Quest musher survives the Arctic environment, as did the original mushers with only their dogs, good looks, wits, and skills.

Drivers start the race with 8 to 14 dogs. They must finish with at least six. The mushers must impeccably care for their dogs. They make all arrangements for the dogs' continued care whether racing or not. No dogs may be added to the team after the race starts.

If a dog is injured, the musher must haul it in the sled in a protected, humane manner. If the racer drops a dog out of the race, all arrangements for its care must be made.

The musher must find a way to repair a broken sled. The Quest requires that the musher must have specific items when checking in. If an item is missing, it must be replaced before going on.

Adverse conditions

Visibility

Whiteout conditions in the mountains disorient even the most experienced. Black, overcast midnights force mushers to travel through darkness that light can't sufficiently penetrate. It shows an act of faith and testifies to the trust placed in the dogs.

Even in calm daylight, storms from the previous night frequently destroy the trail markers. In 1986, Frank loses the trail in a wild storm. He is bogged down on Eagle Summit. Survival dominates his thinking rather than competition. When he gets back on the trail 11 hours later, extensive frostbite marks his face and hands. Experience comes at a cost, and he pays his dues.

Cold

The Yukon Quest takes place in February when the weather is the coldest and least predictable.

The northerners understand the subtleties of subzero weather. When the cold reaches a certain point, it is hard to ice skate. The blade doesn't melt the ice. It is like ice skating on gravel. You can't make a snowman because the snow doesn't melt. It is like making a snowball out of sand.

The dogs cope easily with the cold and the mushers know how to dress for protection. Sometimes, however, debilitating cold threatens to kill cleverly. It first introduces pain and misery, and then begins a slow but increasingly insistent call promising relief if only the body would rest just a little bit.

In the 1996 Quest, Dieter Dolif listens to the siren call. He camps out in the cold for 36 hours, even though a warm checkpoint awaits him two hours away. Hypothermia sets in and disorients him. Race officials send a rescue team.

Fatigue

From the first day, the musher is on the slippery slope of fatigue. Dehydration and monotony hasten the slide. The dry cold air in conjunction with running and climbing makes dehydration more likely. It makes the musher lethargic, possibly dizzy, and disoriented.

Monotony works hand in hand with dehydration. A slow induction of repetitive scenery lulls the musher and diminishes his concentration.

Fatigue waits patiently until the musher blinks, and then blinks again, and then a micro sleep, and perhaps hallucinations compounded by lack of food and water.

Ghostly advice

In 1996, Bill Stewart completes 96% of the race. He is at Takhini Hot Springs, forty miles from the finish. The dogs are in good shape. However, he sees Frank Turner on a small sled with a small dog team.

23

Frank tells Bill, *"This is my own private training trail."* Then Frank adds, *"Besides that, you're going the wrong way."*

Bill turns around and heads the opposite way for four hours. Then he sees Mark May who tells him that he is going the wrong way.

Bill turns around again. Then he meets Larry "Cowboy" Smith who tells him to get a room in the hotel that is over there. Bill stops the team, can't find the hotel, but lies down in the snow in –25° F weather, to rest just a little, just a little.

Luckily, Mark May spots Bill and the stationary team of dogs. He helps Bill push on ahead of him to a third place finish. For his unselfish act the mushers unanimously vote to give Mark the Sportsman Trophy.

In this sequence, Bill does not suspect that Frank is a hallucination. In fact, Frank is several hours behind him. The illusion, however, is as real as the real Mark May. And, Bill cannot differentiate between the real Mark May and his next hallucination, Larry "Cowboy" Smith, who is back in his home in Dawson City.

Hardest Quest ever

The weather is so extreme that the 1986 Quest takes three days longer than expected. A tormenting storm dumps heavy snow and the temperature hovers more than -40° F every day for two weeks. The cold no longer is inconvenient; it is life threatening.

Even the official trail breakers bog down with their snow machines. They break a trail and then re-break the same trail going back in even deeper snow. It is a version of Sisyphus. The labor is futile and the underworld is now blowing snow and frigid cold.

A dozen mushers take turns leading. They break trail almost 700 miles in bitter cold and blinding headwinds.

When the wind gets too severe, they cannot see their dog teams. They can't even see their hands on the driving bow. They cannot drive their dogs from behind; they go to the front to lead them. **In adversity the leader leads.**

Faces and hands freeze, some to the point that they cannot manipulate their fingers to untie their boots. It echoes Jack London's character in *To build a fire*. The prospector freezes to death unable to move his fingers to light a life-saving match:

> The tremendous cold had already driven the life out of his fingers. In his effort to separate one match from the others, the whole bunch fell into the snow. He tried to pick it out of the snow but failed. The dead fingers could neither touch nor clutch. (Jack London, *To build a fire*)

Many are so tired they fall off their sleds, but get back on and keep going. Herd instinct takes over. Nobody wants to travel alone. They move in tandem as a group. The waist-deep snow fatigues even the most experienced. Sonny Lindner, winner of the first Quest in 1984, and Harry Sutherland, the second place finisher, are exhausted.

Bruce Johnson wins the 1986 Quest in 14 days and nine hours. Seven years later, this 20-year veteran of sled dog racing breaks through the ice while on Little Atlin Lake training for the 1993 Quest. Bruce and all his dogs die.

Aesthetics

Extremes are the norm in the Quest. Extreme beauty, emotion, and joy balance the extreme hardships. It is a natural high, not fighting nature but working with it.

The constellations seem close enough to touch, as the northern lights dance to the electromagnetic music of the sun. The sensuous, mystical, vibrant, multicolored lights pulsate, energize, and fascinate. The aurora borealis protects the mushers and dogs.

Isolation does not bring loneliness. Even when Frank is away from the other teams in the race, he is never alone because he has a team of special individuals in front of him.

He knows that the Northern community is with all the mushers, as is he. His competitors are within a couple hundred miles most of the time. Sometimes some mushers are in two places at once, one as a hallucination and one as reality.

Furthermore, various mushers of 22 Quests are with him in

spirit, all heroes, some renegades, all fellow competitors. Like an epic novel, characters dart in and out of his mind with a myriad of stories that give him energy, insight, and grins.

Just as importantly, Frank remembers the names of the other mushers' dogs: Tess and Arrow, Gin Gin, Clovis, Pedro, Bonzo, Milos, and Felix, and Hobo Jim. He has a story for each.

The Quest takes Frank up four mountains where, weather permitting, he scans in crystalline light the whole environment and sees an ever-widening landscape.

He no longer sees just the trees, but the forest and more forests. He no longer sees hills, but clusters of hills and mountains located not on a map but on the land. The startling wholeness imparts a perspective that has its own wisdom.

On the mountain, mushers look ahead and see the next challenge. Occasionally they hear a whisper, "*Give up.*" Momentarily some look behind to where they have been. It doesn't discourage them, but verifies what they can do. They hear a stronger whisper, "*Go on.*"

The aesthetics overwhelm resistance. Feeling dominates thinking. Even the agnostic feels spiritual. Even the tired and weak feel incredibly alive.

Frank's quest

The toughest dog sled race in the world gives Frank a primary goal that is relevant, achievable, and unambiguous. The goal *per se* is not Frank's quest, however. The race is but one of many goals, like fractals, embedded in his bigger quest.

Frank knows where to go and how to get there. Weather, terrain, health of dogs, his health, and countless other factors will challenge the "where" and the "how."

Unknowns lurk between the start and the finish. He doesn't know what he will learn, just that he will learn. He doesn't know how he will be stretched mentally and physically, just that he will be stretched. He doesn't know what will surprise him, just that he will be surprised.

Self-knowledge is the biggest payoff. His most formidable opponent is himself.

The accumulation of Quests provides an unexpected bonus. He sees elements of commonality across the big picture, across compressed time. Like a great wine, Frank's understanding becomes more complex.

Frank jokingly says that every time he enters a Quest he discovers how much he doesn't know. Now, after 22 Quests, he knows nothing.

Like King Arthur's knights searching for the Holy Grail, like the pilgrims in the *Canterbury Tales*, like Siddartha searching for truth, the journey confirms the expected and whimsically introduces the unexpected.

Many will not make it to the finish line, but in the process discover something about their ego, physical limitations, strength, spirituality, convictions, identity, conviviality, and their dogs.

Jack London projects that the white silence of the north forces the traveler to a spiritual reckoning:

> All movement ceases, the sky clears, the heavens are as brass; the slightest whisper seems sacrilege, and man becomes timid, affrighted at the sound of his own voice. Sole speck of life journeying across the ghostly wastes of a dead world, he trembles at his audacity, realizes that his is a maggot's life, nothing more.

> Strange thoughts arise unsummoned, and the mystery of all things strives for utterance. And the fear of death, of God, of the universe, comes over him—the hope of the Resurrection and the Life, the yearning for immortality, the vain striving of the imprisoned essence—it is then, if ever, man walks alone with God. (Jack London, *The White Silence*)

Contrary to London's conclusion, Frank does not feel he is walking alone. Fear is not the primary emotion. Awe, and a sense of running a race with and for the community, dominates more.

Building on his love for dogs, he helps communities, shapes opportunities for young people, serves national and international visitors, works with professionals and raises an extended family.

They, in turn, celebrate and affirm his life, satisfying the yearning for reassurance.

Frank's worthy quest goes beyond the dogsled race. When he runs a Quest, a mythic ritual plays out that affirms his and the community's core values. The unfolding drama yields both personal and archetypal meaning.

Just as the journey in the *Wizard of Oz* paradoxically and dramatically demonstrates to the Cowardly Lion, Tin Woodman, Scarecrow, and Dorothy that they have the answers and have had them all along, the Yukon Quest creates conditions where self-knowledge can win over self-doubt.

Essence of worthy quests

The motivating impact of a worthy quest is so powerful that every person should devote inordinate attention to it. **A worthy quest is magical.** It marshals energy, lights fires in the belly, and affirms life.

Don Quixote, a 16th century fictional character, the delusional man from La Mancha, intuitively understands the need to create, conjure up, and declare a quest. When he sets out, the destination is unknown, but the need to "search" compels.

And—here is his insight—he creates a reason to search. Thus, the beautiful Dulcinea emerges from his fertile imagination.

In his quest, Quixote passionately fights imagined giants, battles armies and frees gentlemen.

> Oh Dulcinea de Tobosa, day of my night, glory of my suffering, true North and compass of every path I take, guiding star of my fate . . . (Miguel de Cervantes, *Don Quixote*)

The Man from La Mancha passionately lives a life of discovery even though every event can be cast as a failure. **Out of nothing, god-like, he creates a quest and a reason to passionately pursue it.**

The process occurs for countless other individuals who dare to dream: Jack London, John Kennedy, Sir Edmund Hillary and Tenzing Norgay, and Frank Turner.

London blinks and writes 51 books. Kennedy blinks and America lands on the moon. Hillary and Tenzing blink and Mt. Everest yields. Turner blinks and 22 Quests pass.

You don't need a huge goal. And, remember goals follow goals. Frequently, parallel goals occur. Consider both private and public, short-term and long-term goals. The goals along with the processes to get there, taken together, are part of your worthy quest. Craft something that suits you.

Task #1 for passionate leaders

The first task for passionate leaders is to get a quest that entails a well-defined goal. People need a "Fairbanks" to go to.

A company without a quest can neither energize nor focus its employees or managers. This point became very vivid recently while working with one of my clients.

Aimless sailing

The managing director of a steel manufacturing company is a bundle of contradictions. Personally, he accepts a sailing quest. He wants to master nautical skills. As part of the quest, he sails in the annual Sydney to Hobart Yacht Race.

High performance crews average about two days to sail 630 nautical miles through notoriously dangerous seas. At a strategic planning session for his senior managers, I ask him three questions. *"What is your company's worthy quest? Where is your company's Hobart? What are your company's goals entailed by the quest?"*

He cannot answer any of the questions and neither can his employees. He says, *"We just go out and sail leisurely around the harbor and make money."*

For the past five years, however, they find less and less wind. They lose market leadership across the six products that previously give them 90% of their profit. Now they chase dozens of smaller products that the leaders ignore. The company's growth hovers around 1%, while the leading competitors speed along in cyclonic winds.

Last year, they make money because a dishonest supplier compromises the standards of their competitors, who are then forced to recall products.

Oddly, the owner of this "questless" company brags about his successful year, ignoring the aberrations. His senior managers are nervous.

They don't argue for a worthy quest. Instead, they offer hackneyed, financial goals interchangeable with any company. Their goals are laissez-faire, after the fact, non-motivating, certainly not life affirming, more life squirming, not guaranteed to foster insight, growth, or self-discovery.

Do it now

A person with Alzheimer's disease lives in the ever present now, and so do you. The difference is that a future beckons you. The gap between the future and now creates a tension and sets up a comparison. What will change between then and now?

Will you blink your eyes and only notice time has passed? Or, will you commit to a worthy quest now, blink your eyes, and see consequences? A quest will change your life.

All quests need goals. The goal may be at a high level of abstraction, maybe to simply search and learn. Or, it may be very specific—build a company, survive cancer, or get children through college.

Distractions and procrastination

Distractions, procrastination, and absence of will prevent people from getting a quest. Frivolous activity that requires a small expenditure of energy often competes for your attention.

My friend, J.M., complains that he has no time to make an extra effort to obtain a passive income, potentially one of his quests.

Yet, he habitually watches television four hours daily, a narcotic mix of local news, cricket, and the comedy channel. This seemingly minor pattern amounts to 28 hours per week, 1456 per year, or 61 full 24-hour days of passive activity. He blinks and 23,000 commercials have passed.

In contrast, when my grandfather retires at the age of 65, I offer to teach him to play chess. He says he doesn't want to learn at his age, but humors me. He ends up playing for 15 years including multiple postal chess games before his death. He blinks and becomes a chess enthusiast.

Two years ago, my friend Ben, who has no experience in art, wants to become an art dealer. He works backwards from the goal. He can't analyze the art market and competition until he understands his personal interests and needs. He doesn't fully understand his personal interests until he spends time visiting galleries, looking at art books, and talking to artists.

As Ben accomplishes each minor goal, his understanding deepens and his vision sharpens. When an art gallery comes on the market, Ben jumps at the opportunity. He does not struggle with the decision. Now, he is on a steep learning curve, and I have not seen him happier or less stressed.

At the age of 57, I begin riding a motorcycle. I fear for my life in the early training. Since then, I have ridden many trips including 4000 miles from Montana to Alaska and back, and have written a book about it. It is a journey about fathers coming to grips, discovering, and coping with sons and daughters. Profound emotions, hidden memories, and unfinished business emerge. It redirects my life.

Communicate your passion

Don't be afraid to passionately and persuasively communicate your quest to the people you care about. Being secretive about information does damage in several ways. First, people always fill a vacuum, often leaning toward the most negative interpretation.

Second, people perceive withholding information as game playing, and frequently, it is seen as mean spirited. Information vacuums alienate individuals.

Sharing information, especially related to big objectives, quests, or core philosophies is part of treating them right.

Furthermore, if they are employees, it catches their imaginations, and positions them to contribute beyond job descriptions. If the quest is a worthy one, individuals work better, awaken sleeping talents, and build on experiential successes. It electrifies the company.

So, **get a worthy quest!** It can be for you, your family, or organization. The worthy quest makes you learn and grow. It positions you to be surprised, pleased, and frequently awed.

chapter two

Give life to your values!

Enchanting Yukon

Muktuk Kennels sits in a historic location touched by an astrological event. The Chikats, one of the First Nation Clans in the Northwest, guard the knowledge of the Yukon interior for hundreds of years.

In 1869, George Davidson, an American scientist, travels up the Chikat River. He meets Kohklux, leader of the wolf clan, and tells him about the imminent solar eclipse. The successful prediction impresses him so much, he accepts Davidson as a friend and agrees to share his knowledge with him.

The First Nation Chief and his two wives, in three days, draw an incredible map that shows major lakes, rivers, three dimensional views of mountains, settlements, campsites, the main inland trading route, significant landmarks, and events and details about living conditions. They measure distances in travel time.

Kohklux's historic map, which precisely describes lakes, rapids, and rivers around the Whitehorse area, matches features from satellite photography.

Muktuk Kennels can accurately be placed on the ancient map.

The northern environment projects its own values; maybe it's my subconscious. The trees and bushes whisper, *"Live in balance, in peace."* The air urges deep, clean breaths: *"Enjoy life now."* The water, some calm, some rambunctious, some icy cold, some boiling hot, signals change and no change at the same time: *"Be perplexed. Be in awe."* The crows, hawks, and eagles, first fascinate with their graceful ease, then tease, *"Fly, if you can, if you dare."*

Frank's values

Frank proudly declares his values to anybody who will listen. He puts them on his business brochures, weaves them into his educational talks and introduces them on his website homepage. *Muktuk is a place for people who love dogs:*

> **Dogs First!** We are dedicated to providing the best possible care for our dogs, considering their physical, emotional, psychological and social needs. Our relationship with our dogs involves focusing on the quality of every single thing that happens between us. Simply, we always put our dogs first! (www.muktuk.com)

Everything builds on this premise.

However, these values are hollow and hypocritical if the dogs are unhappy. My first training run in the morning with the dogs would reveal much. The dogs can't lie.

Dog training

The next day, ice crystals flicker in the 14° F air at Muktuk. Frost covers the spruce and pine trees and blankets the fields. Clouds hide the mountaintop.

Frank secures the 4-wheel Honda All Terrain Vehicle (ATV) to a post with a rope. If he doesn't anchor the ATV, the dogs run away with it. A dog sled replaces the ATV when enough snow covers the trails.

He lays out enough towline for seven pairs of dogs. Over a hundred dogs bark to get Frank's attention. The dogs in the front rows are the most insistent. *"Take me, take me!"*

They strain at their chains, jump up on their hind legs, and paw the air. They race back and forth or around their doghouses, some jump on top of the houses. *"Take me, take me!"*

If a dog does not want to go on the run, Frank knows the individual well enough to find out if there is a physical, emotional, or psychological problem. The physical part is the easiest to deal with. The trickier problem is to understand the mental processes of the dog.

When Frank lays a harness in front of a dog, the dog knows that a run is imminent. It is going to be a great day. The chosen dogs often stop barking and lie next to the harness while the rest of the dogs continue their clamor.

He harnesses the lead dog first, slipping the head and front legs through the nylon straps. He lifts the dog to its back legs so that the powerful front legs are controlled. He walks or hops the dog to the first position in the towline.

Frank clips the lead dog into the tow and instructs the dog to stay. The dog momentarily suppresses exploding energy. It's like giving a child a piece of candy, but saying not to eat it just yet.

He hooks up a younger lead dog next to the first dog, and instructs it to stay. Both dogs lie side by side. They glance around like they are ready to jump out of their skins.

By the time he hooks six dogs, they pull at the towline in uncoordinated lurches, moving the ATV and shaking the post it is anchored to. He hooks up eight more dogs. The rope seems increasingly inadequate to hold the ATV.

The dogs on the towline bark incessantly now. They are loud and insistent. They want to run. The other dogs in the yard bark support.

When one of the dog handlers releases the rope, the dogs awkwardly jerk the ATV forward, but they quickly settle into a smooth motion as 56 feet adjust to each other's rhythm.

As the dog team leaves, a silence descends on the dog yard so

Frank gives educational talks to about 500 people every summer, visiting from over 20 countries. Hershel, Livingston, and Ella help. (Color plate 1)

Muktuk Kennels sits on the Takhini River just outside Whitehorse, Yukon. It is the home to over 100 dogs, including puppies and rescued dogs. (Color plate 2)

Heidi plays with Marie from Quebec and Rob from Australia during the daily program. The dog handlers feed and water the dogs, keep their areas clean, and exercise and play with them. (Color plate 3)

Frank's weathered hands tenderly hold two of Beethoven's pups. The Canadian Broadcast Corporation held a contest to name the pups. Frank's staff discussed and voted on the names. (Color plate 4)

Dogs are a source of conversation, but good stories, politics, current affairs, trivia, and philosophies are not far behind. Brenda from Finland, Anne, Frank and Saul, his son, are shown. (Color plate 5)

The Aurora Borealis dances over Circle, Alaska. Dick Hutchinson has photographed the northern lights for over two decades. His website offers photographic tips and presents an excellent sampling of his work. (Color plate 6)

Edith Jerome immortalized the Yukon River, in a mural, *White Horse Rapids*, on the side of the MacBride Museum in Whitehorse. The river claimed over 200 lives in the summer of 1898. Jack London guided boats down the rapids a few times. (Color plate 7)

Frank entertains at the 2005 Yukon Quest Banquet. Stories about mushing, earlier Quests and northern life blend seamlessly. Frank is a born story teller and loves the conviviality. (Color plate 8)

Race starts are explosive. Dogs strain on the towline in anticipation of starting the race. The lead dogs almost levitate in their enthusiasm. It takes many handlers to hold them. (Color plate 9)

Frank and his team head to Dawson. The lead dogs focus on the trail. Each knows their job, In the early part of the race, they need to find their rhythm. (Color plate 10)

The dogs' needs come before Frank's. At rest stops, he prepares straw beds, to maintain the dogs' body heat in readiness for the next leg. He checks their physical well being. He also notes their moods and attitudes. (Color plate 11)

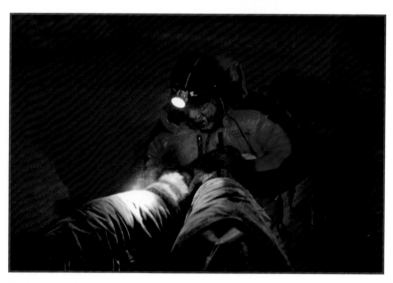

Frank congratulates his dogs for a job well done–getting to Dawson. They have run through the night. His team knows their efforts are appreciated. He talks to each dog individually attending to the dog's particular personality. (Color plate 12)

Frank's dogs get five-star hospitality in Dawson City during the mandatory 36-hour layover. They have just run 500 miles. Anne orchestrates the operation with both nurturing and discipline. (Color plate 13)

Synchronization and determination show as the team covers miles of terrain in magically beautiful, yet unforgiving conditions. The river is always a potential threat. Frank must read the conditions impeccably. (Color plate 14).

When everything is right, it sounds as though only one set of paws hit the trail. Everything is in harmony. Frank is now working with a high performance team. (Color plate 15)

Anne's organizational skills and solid support complement Frank's and the dogs' efforts to successfully run the Yukon Quest. Others frequently point to Muktuk's operation as a model. (Color plate 16)

quickly that it is startling. No dog barks. All look wistfully in the direction of the dog team. *"Maybe next time."*

Even before the dogs round the last curve to the finish, the Muktuk dogs are on their feet welcoming them back. They have been gone one hour, up and down five steep hills, around sharp turns, and through nine miles of Yukon forest.

After the run, the dogs lie on the ground to rest and Frank is on the ground. He talks to each dog, touches them, looks them in the eyes and lets them see his soul.

Then he gives them a mixture of food and water. Each dog gets a personal bowl.

The training mimics the race itself. All the excitement is at the beginning. If something goes wrong, it usually occurs in the initial period. Fairly quickly things settle down and the team searches for its rhythm.

It is not a question of whether something will go wrong, but only a question of when. Then the only thing that makes a difference is how the musher handles it. This is the difference between success and failure. Trouble is often the better teacher.

Essentially, the dogs testify to the quality of Frank's care. They are happy, healthy dogs who want to run. He is among three Quest mushers who have won the Veterinarian's Award twice for the most humane treatment and overall care for his or her dogs throughout the year. He wins it in 1991 and then wins it a decade later.

Working values

Frank doesn't buy dog teams; he raises them from puppies. The bonding begins early. He and his staff play with them, fawn over them, and monitor their health. They nurture, train, and develop dogs with a single-minded focus: to raise happy, healthy dogs.

Puppies are important at Muktuk. The staff dotes on them. For Beethoven's last litter, the Canadian Broadcasting Corporation holds a nationwide contest to name each puppy. The father is Schubert. Hundreds of listeners suggest names ranging from puns (Wagging-er, Bark-rowk, J. S. Bark, Tchi-arf-ski) to the most frequently nominated name, Wolfgang.

The staff debates, lobbies, and then chooses the names at dinner: Rimsky, Aida, Vivaldi, Opus, and Wolfgang. Tragically, soon after the puppies are named, they fight for their lives. A parasite has invaded their bodies.

Many kennels cull their dogs if they fail to show speed, strength, or endurance. They cull them if they show a defect, get too sick, or recover from an injury too slowly.

In a world where dog racing increasingly forces kennels to make business decisions relating to breed or competition, they sell the weak dogs, or in some instances shoot them. In this world where the fittest survive not by nature but by man, Frank stands out.

Frank refuses to cull his dogs. If they are injured, he nurses them back to health. One of Frank's 1995 Quest winning dogs, Wally, has advanced cancer. So does Pinocchio, a sweet female dog. He cares for them until they die. They do not have to be the strongest or fastest to remain part of the Muktuk community.

In 1986, he takes in 30 abandoned dogs at a great expense to Muktuk, and at considerable legal harassment from an overzealous bankruptcy litigator.

He finds homes for 13 dogs. He names the remaining animals his "rescue dogs." Simi, one of the guides from Germany, takes a special interest in them. They form their own team. They now race in short distance contests.

Buck is lead dog in Frank's 1995 winning Quest. Buck now has house privileges.

Personal attention

Frank personally feeds and waters the dogs he trains. All Muktuk dogs get a customized diet, including vitamins, based on Frank's nutritional research.

He likes alternative health approaches. The dogs get acupressure, and in some instances acupuncture. Also, they routinely get homeopathic and naturopathic medicines, as well as chiropractic and physiotherapeutic treatments.

Each dog has its own shelter, a 2 x 2 x 3 foot doghouse with dry straw and a small opening to protect him or her from the weather. The dog shuts out extremely cold weather by putting its back to the door.

His support team keeps fresh straw in the doghouses and twice a day the guides go on "poop scoop" duty to assure a hygienic environment. They examine the dogs' feces, note how they eat, and inspect paws.

He vaccinates and deworms them. He attends to their injuries and works closely with veterinarians. Often a dog has sore muscles. Marie, a 20-year-old blond guide from Quebec, and Fabian, a 23-year-old brunette guide from Switzerland, simultaneously massage the dog and give new meaning to the phrase "lucky dog."

The dogs, who work hard, especially in the winter, need to have lots of fun during the down time. Play, even for the older dogs, is essential. Play and work are in balance.

In the summer, the staff keeps the dogs cool with adequate shade, water, and river walks. All dogs participate, not just the Quest contenders. Periodically, they release two dozen dogs to run around the trails parallel to the Takhini River.

health. He knows the idiosyncrasies of Decaf, Terror, Buck, Livingston, Stanley, Latte, and Herschel. He talks to them personally. They understand his tone, rhythm, and pattern of attention.

Conversely, the dogs sense the musher's emotional health. They know when Frank is happy or sad, healthy or sick, energetic or tired. The dogs are extraordinarily intuitive.

Frank habitually kneels, talks and hugs the dogs. He coos to them. He repeats their names lovingly. He talks to each like a soul mate.

Anne Tayler, his partner, could leave him in a second, pointing to countless communicative intimacies outside the marriage; except, she understands these intimacies, and she does the same thing. They are a simpatico team.

More than a business

Frank's operation transcends a dog business. It has become an "ideal." He is a Canadian national treasure, a jewel in the crown of Canadian superlatives, founded on consistent, living, demonstrated values.

Extended family

Every night the dinner table is a conversational smorgasbord. It is like multiple *Dinners with Andre*. Dogs dominate the discussions, but every topic is up for grabs with multiple, international perspectives. The conversations are lively, rapid, and congenial.

After each training run, he asks the staff what they learned. *Where is the towline slack? What is their gait like? Are they eating? How is their attitude? Who likes the hills?* And, perhaps the best question of all: *What did they learn about themselves?*

In the house, Frank intuitively uses questions to teach. Outside, even though he may not be able to explain some things, he teaches by example. He is an intuitive, patient teacher. Even the most mundane jobs are seen as opportunities to interact with the dogs. Zen moments.

Aspiring guides from around the world apply to be part of Muktuk as apprentices. They learn how to care for, train, and run dogs. They have to accept the values that lie behind Frank's methods. Their learning entails taking visitors on dogsleds to see the raw beauty of the Yukon in the Canadian winter.

And, they provide operational support for Frank during the Quest. They work like an Indianapolis 500 ground crew. They know their roles, efficiently carry them out, and monitor the dogs' total well-being. Race officials point to Frank's operation as an ideal in dog care.

Frank's philosophy forges itself on their consciousness. His staff shares the same values, infected by Frank's enthusiasm. **Frank treats his people like dogs**.

Each summer about 500 visitors from over 20 countries hear Frank talk about the Quest and his dogs. The international visitors interact with and walk with the dogs.

Their exuberance is infectious. Energy levels soar. The visitors smile and laugh. They pick favorite dogs to feed. They leave Muktuk with a huge understanding of his stewardship. Frank's weakness is that he can't stop talking about the dogs. A two-hour talk slips into a four or five hour visit.

Context of values

Frank is explicit when he says he gets so much from the dogs: *"They define who I am, what I do and how I behave. The dogs have saved my life. They have taken me through adversity. They have given me purpose. They teach me continually."*

They motivate him, make him feel alive and confident, and anchor him. He does not have to rethink moral implications.

By valuing the dogs so much, Frank finds reassurance for himself. By putting his faith in his team, he puts faith in himself. It is a Buddhist-like trick that calms and centers him.

It is deceptive to think that Frank simply loves dogs. He loves the Alaskan bred dogs. These are not Greyhound racing dogs bred to chase a mechanical rabbit around an oblong racing track. These are not show dogs trying to win best in class. These are not attack police dogs.

They are dogs from the land. They are the dogs that Jack London saw and wrote about in *The call of the wild* and *White Fang*. **These dogs link the northern wilderness and man**.

Environmental shaping

The mountains, weather, and light bring their values. The mountains deliberately mix their messages like mystical teachers. On the gentle side, they softly sing like a lullaby, "*Be comfortable. Feel protected and nurtured.*" Although the mountains sustain some, they scare others. Some Indian Nations leave the mountains because they hear spirits whispering. Other Nations stay for the same reason; whispering spirits connect them to nature.

The mountains, some snow capped all year, remind humans of their size, if nothing else, a speck in the landscape. They conjure grandeur and forces bigger, much bigger, than the person. They insistently nudge the individual to reflect.

The weather works similarly but often without the subtleness of the sublime. A 30-degree drop catches the attention of the most stubborn. A snowstorm where you cannot see your hand in front of your face demands perspective taking.

The weather tells you, until you absolutely believe it, change will come, and come again, and again. With change, both newness and sameness, like an oriental riddle, force learning. Heraclites is alive and well: You cannot step into the same stream twice (Plato, *Cratylus* 402A).

And then, . . . and then there's the relationship of light to the Yukon. All year it dances a balance between the land of the midnight sun in the summer and short days in the winter urging that one notice change.

And, if that is not enough, the northern lights mystically, romantically, and hauntingly tantalize even the most obstinate agnostic with unearthly mysteries.

It is difficult to imagine people celebrating the mid-west experience on the windy plains of Alberta or the flats of Salt Lake City with the same intensity or salience. But Yukoners lose their "selves" in the Northern experience, caught by either confusion or enlightenment. Many searchers despair, others soar. The broken hearted find hope, . . . sometimes . . . often times.

The dogs that Frank values simultaneously link him to the environment and to the northern history. But his biggest need links him to something else—he wants reassurance.

Need for reassurance

Frank says that he is most like his dog, Livingston, not his lead dogs like Buck, Decaf, or Stanley. It is an insightful analysis. Livingston leads with the best, but needs to have reassurance. With this comparison, he gives the key to how to understand him, and how he understands his dogs, not just Livingston.

Believable, timely, and realistic reassurance is the key. The pattern comes from his mother, who was overly protective. He remembers a pivotal moment in his life. At 26 years of age, he realizes that his father's DNA is not the cause of any of his problems. This epiphany forces an existential imperative on him.

He chooses sociology for his career path, a discipline lodged in reassurance. He cites Herman Hesse (*Siddartha*), Saul Alinsky (*Rules for Radicals*), and Richard Bach (*Johnathan Livingston Seagull*) as influences from his studies.

Frank laments that none of his classmates ever visit him. It is a surprising disclosure and a telling one. Also, Frank reports that his first wife never congratulated or celebrated his Quest contests. Eventually she demands that he decide between her and the dogs.

The fire in Frank's voice reflects the values he lives. He says what is in his heart.

He may not be aware of it, but he practices the *I-Thou* philosophy championed by the Jewish existentialist, Martin Buber. When he communicates, he brings his whole being to encounters whether with animals or humans.

Frank does something more complicated than valuing dogs, who, in turn, value him. Here's the Buddhist-like trick again. He fosters communities that value both dogs and people who value dogs.

As a consequence, his extended family, the Yukon community, northern community, and Quest community ultimately reassure Frank. He activates communities and makes a difference.

Frank's values are not like dusty rocks lying on a road getting in the way. They are like cascading rapids that rush down a river affecting everything in their path.

They show themselves most when crashing over obstacles. He rescues 30 dogs he can't afford to keep, but does so anyway. He advocates a special award for volunteers of the Yukon Quest in memory of a tragically killed musher. He lobbies government for fair treatment of landowners.

Task #2 for passionate leaders

Passionate leaders give life to their values. The values don't lie dead in the obligatory corporate mission statement, waiting like zombies to be resurrected by catastrophic events, unexpected media attention, or overly zealous, dissatisfied customers.

Leaders know what they believe and prefer, and they commend their values to others. The commitment entails both apparent and hidden consequences.

There is little room for grayness. People know which side of the fence the person sits. The certainty of an unambiguous position carries its strength. The statement "*I believe and accept this value*" is powerful.

Parents who effectively and unambiguously model and craft values for their children, raise resilient individuals. By the time children grow up, the values should be sufficiently robust and consistent to withstand spur of the moment assaults, tests, and whimsical deviations. The values cascade through generations.

Employees drive values

Leaders who effectively communicate viable values in an organization do not have to drive them. The employees do. They influence everybody in their work place. When an extortionist threatens a large, privately owned pharmaceutical company, the company stops production. Three hundred employees face unemployment.

The founder and CEO, assembles all employees and explains the situation. He tells them that he does not know how, but he will not lay off any person.

A line worker yells, *"We are with you, Paul."* Every worker comes to work, even without pay, to see the crisis through.

Just as Frank refuses to cull dogs, Paul refuses to cull workers in a crisis. They will survive together or fall together.

Paul has no need to cajole employees to accept certain values. Instead, they live and drive the values themselves. They do not need the whining exhortations of company newsletters, emails, or communiqués to behave in certain ways.

In absence of values

Daily behaviors of people in a company, like a weather system, are a whirl of morals. Employees read the company currents like an experienced sailor. Double standards, unfair dismissals, heavy handed control, and tolerated bad behavior show what the company values.

In the absence of either a worthy quest or accepted values, employees fill the vacuum with activity. They first protect their jobs with razor sharp skills that focus on their needs. These activities will not sustain the company.

Three marketers in a San Francisco fruit drink company have no idea where the company wants to go or why— no quest, no values. Activity doesn't stop; it increases. They create meaningless work to protect their jobs.

They spend a year repackaging a range of commodity products. They solicit three tenders from graphic artists, debate the aesthetics of each proposed labeling over several months, fight over fonts, secure association approval, present new labels to the trade, and launch the newly labeled products.

Ironically, the CEO awards the team with a plaque recognizing the team's hard work. Market share does not change after the launch. Consumers continue to buy the products on price, and price alone.

Devoid of values, the company misses many opportunities. The accountant's books never reveal the magnitude of losses. The company suffers without knowing why.

When an organization fails to give life to its values, they tacitly give employees permission to be apathetic. The tipping point comes when employees conclude that the company does not care about them, like a bad relationship, they find it easy to not care about the company.

In presence of values

Company actions demonstrate more than company rhetoric that values live in employees. Just as Frank's dogs don't hide their eagerness to run, employees who know that their company lives its values don't hide their enthusiasm.

IKEA employees, for example, like their company and work. The company lives its values by providing comprehensive benefits including:

- Full time medical and dental insurance for those working 20 hours or more per week. Eligibility extends to domestic partners and children. Those working less than 20 hours also have access to full benefits.
- Discounts for weight loss and smoking cessation programs.
- Free subscriptions to health and wellness magazines.
- Flexible work arrangements including job share, telecommuting, coordinated work schedules, and condensed work weeks.

- Paid maternity/paternity leave.

- Paid time-off for child adoption.

- Tuition assistance for graduate and undergraduate degrees. A $1000 bonus if the degree is completed while working at IKEA.

- Quiet rooms, recreation rooms, lactation rooms and a comfortable and entertaining room area for employees' family members to enjoy when visiting.

- Deeply discounted hot and cold meals at IKEA restaurants.

- Two to five weeks paid vacation per year, based on length of service. Vacation time may be carried over into the next year.

- Extensive professional development and training programs.

The above benefits are not gimmicks, but economic realities that impact both employees and the company. For instance, IKEA saves millions of dollars in recruiting and retention retraining cost. IKEA regularly makes the top 100 best companies to work for.

Passionate leaders embrace sustainable values that cascade through the lives of others. They make a difference. Frank's values do not change because of arbitrary events or tough times. The values are sustainable and well-communicated. They cascade through his family, business, and community. The dogs' energy, health, and attitude reflect what Frank lives.

It is easy to list values for a company policy or a personal declaration. It is harder to live them, get them under your skin and into your consciousness. Others should see the result of living values as a consequence. Like the Yukon rapids, they should affect everyone in their path.

chapter three

Get the right dogs in the right jobs!

First walk among the dogs

The first time I walk among the dogs at Muktuk they watch me intensely. They try to catch my eye. *Do they know I am Frank's friend?*

Some raise their paw and draw it vertically down as though against an invisible glass. *Do they know Marcel Marceau?* I feel an urge to reach out. *Am I supposed to shake hands, shake paws?*

Many wag their tails like they've had too much caffeine. Others jump on their hind legs with only their chains holding them back, standing almost as tall as I am. Still others jump to the top of their doghouses to get eye level with me. Some play coy or feign indifference.

Most try to engage. Each dog has its own style, its own tricks.

Do I greet all 110 dogs or selectively talk to some dogs. I choose the latter, but now I must make more choices. *Do I engage with the ones who seem to most want to engage me? Do I approach the ones resisting my presence, the more challenging ones? Do I spend time with the more lonely, forlorn, or jaded? Will the others feel slighted?*

They thrive on affection. Some demand it. They look into my eyes. A few scan to see whether I have a snack. There is no shyness here. They are not shifty-eyed. I wonder about their third eye lid underneath the outer two, the one that cleanses their eye.

The shape and color of their eyes individualize them to the point that I think, *"You're the comedian, and you're Mr. Cynic, and you're a bit of a Sad Sack, and you're the optimist."*

I am not used to unbroken eye contact, quite the contrary, people often point out my lack of eye contact. The dogs know this. This realization is disconcerting. One dog has ghost eyes with white irises. I would have named him Dracula instead of Dutch.

Sense of smell

All I smell is the dog yard, but they smell a million things about me. Dogs have about 25 times more olfactory receptors than we do. They sense odors at concentrations nearly 100 million times lower than we can. They can detect one drop of blood in five quarts of water.

Wild canines rely on smell to hunt. The wind and air currents are their version of wireless technology. They decode information from scents to determine friends and foes, predators and prey. On dog sled runs, the dogs react to rabbits, moose, and wolves invisible to the musher but obvious to the dogs.

Because of their keen sense of smell, dogs can track trails and lost humans, rescue avalanche victims, and detect drugs, bombs, and bodies.

If odors were visible, we would see a kaleidoscope of colors and shapes each with bits of information overlapping and bumping into each other. As humans, we miss these intersecting and changing messages; the dogs don't.

Sense of hearing

They hear fainter sounds than I do. They hear across greater distances than I do. They locate the direction of the sound better by pricking and swiveling their open, funnel shaped ears to scan the environment.

They hear things that I cannot within a range of 67 Hz to 45 kHz. I do not hear high-pitched sounds, the squealing of a small animal or screech of a bird. I only hear between 16 Hz to 20 kHz.

The dogs are extremely sensitive to a human's voice as it changes tone, pitch, and tremor. They react accordingly. The way the mushers talk to their dogs is an art.

When I was eight years old, I cut across a junkyard. Suddenly a half dozen chow dogs attack me. The owner saves me. I do not know whether they would have hurt me, but I am leery, maybe fearful of packs of dogs.

Now walking through their yard I remember my attack and the

hairs on the back of my neck stand up. These dogs know it, but welcome me nevertheless.

So with their eye contact, sense of smell, and sense of hearing, I am totally transparent. Thank God they don't talk the way humans do, excluding Lassie and Rin Tin Tin, of course.

Periodically, through the day and night the whole yard sings. I don't know who cues them. Some howl, some bark and howl. Others do solos.

The performance lasts as long as a song. Then the whole yard goes abruptly quiet. They know the call of the wild well.

> With the aurora borealis flaming coldly overhead, the stars leaping in the frost dance, the land numb and frozen under its pall of snow, this song of the huskies might have been the defiance of life, only it was pitched in minor key, with long-drawn wailings and half–sobs, and was more the pleading of life . . . . It was an old song. (Jack London, *The call of the wild*)

Partnership with dogs

Before Muktuk there are a thousand yesterdays. Over 4000 years ago, the Native people in the frozen tundra of North America domesticate direct descendants of wolves by whatever means necessary.

These village dogs are the first to form the dog-man relationship. From the earliest days, all kinds of dogs make life easier for man. Dogs like Stickeen, Julian, Balto, and Baldy become legends.

In 1880, John Muir, the founder of the Sierra Club, takes Stickeen, a rare Tahltahn Bear Dog, standing about 14 inches high, to explore a glacier in Southeast Alaska.

A deep and forbidding crevice traps them. The only way to safety is over a tenuously thin, knife-edged ice bridge spanning the deadly gulf.

First, Muir digs a set of ice steps down to the bridge.

Stickeen crosses the biggest bridge of his life.

Then, he edges across, straddling both sides of the sliver of ice with his legs. When he gets across, he calls to Stickeen.

After much delay, and clear apprehension, Stickeen finally eases over the ice bridge:

> . . . finally in despair he hushed his cries, slid his little feet slowly down into my footsteps out on the big sliver, walked slowly and cautiously along the sliver as if holding his breath, while the snow was falling and the wind was moaning and threatening to blow him off . (John Muir, *Stickeen*)

When he gets to the other side, he leaps up the ice steps, and rolls in the snow over and over. Muir takes over a decade to write the story, but when he does, it becomes one of the most famous dog stories of the era.

Tappan Adney photographed these working dogs in 1900.

What convinced him to do it? Did he have an internal conversation with himself? *You can do it. Don't look down. Careful, don't slip. One step at a time.* His mind-boggling courage places him among the legendary Yukon dogs.

Day-to-day Yukon dogs pull lumber, cordwood, logs and supplies in the winter. They carry small loads on their backs in the summer.

At the height of the gold rush, over 1500 dogs live in Dawson City. Every third or fourth person owns a dog. In 1900, Tappan Adney, a journalist and accomplished photographer, travels to the Yukon and writes the *Klondike Stampede*. The book contains 125 pictures. There are 91 dogs in the photos.

Northerners like the dual nature of dogs. First, they like the beast in the dog. London foreshadows Buck's transition from domesticated to wild with an ancient song that the title, *The call of the wild*, epitomizes. Buck wakes up one night:

> From the forest came the call (or one note of it, for the call was many-noted), distinct and definite as never before—a long-drawn howl, like, yet unlike, any noise made by the husky dog. And he knew it, in the old familiar way, as a sound heard before. (Jack London, *The call of the wild*)

The beast in the dogs links the mushers to the wild. The same primordial call that stirs the dogs, also beckons the adventurers to accept a quest.

Second, people like the social side in the dog. John Schandelmeir, 1992 and 1996 Yukon Quest winner, recounts the story for the mushers at the 2005 Yukon Quest banquet: *In ancient times a giant crevice in the ice separated all the wild animals from man. The dog saw the crevice and raced to it and jumped across to be with man. He has been with us ever since.*

Dog owners like the dog's unconditional regard, authentic affection, and the straightforward, unmanaged communication. They do not have to guess whether the dog likes them. The dog's tail, eyes, and demeanor show it all with no hint of game playing. The owners are the be all and end all for the dogs. The regard and subsequent bonding last longer than many marriages.

For this reason, northerners value a dog's companionship more than the dog's work, especially during the long winters when the tilt of the earth shortens days to four or five hours, when cabin fever hovers like a disease.

Super athletes

Alaskan dogs can't run as fast as the cheetah, which runs 70 miles per hour. They don't have the endurance of the Arctic tern, which flies 22,000 miles round trip from Antarctica annually. They lack the strength of the rhinoceros beetle, which can lift 850 times its own weight. But taken together, their speed, strength, and endurance put them among the world's best athletes.

Speed

The fastest human runs about 23 miles per hour for a short distance of 328 feet. A middle distance runner (6+ miles) slows to about 18 miles per hour and a marathon runner slows to about 12 miles per hour for 26 miles, 319 yards. By comparison, a dog team runs 18 to 20 miles per hour for a short distance, namely 4 to 20 miles. A middle distance dog team slows to 15 to 17 miles per hour in races between 20 and 100 miles in length.

Essentially, they run as fast as the world record holder for the

400-meter sprint for short distances. Moreover, they can keep a fast pace up for four to five hours, rest, and then do it again. Their overall average is five miles per hour in a rest-run cycle.

Endurance

Dog teams not only run fast, even in adverse conditions, but run for a long time. A long distance dog team averages 14 miles per hour in the run cycle for races from 100 to 1200 miles.

After Buck becomes lead dog in *The call of the wild*, they make record runs:

> In one run they made a sixty-mile dash from the foot of Lake Laberge to the Whitehorse Rapids. Across Marsh, Tagish, and Bennett (seventy miles of lakes), they flew so fast that the man whose turn it was to run towed behind the sled at the end of a rope. (Jack London, *The call of the wild*)

Lance Armstrong burns 5200 calories a day during the 21 days of cycling in the Tour de France. A dog, one third the weight, consumes 8,000 to 10,000 calories per day during the Quest. Pound for pound, a dog consumes six or seven times more energy.

At the same time, they perform at higher efficiency. They have more mitochondria in their cells and more blood vessels bring oxygen to the cells. And, they have relatively bigger hearts.

The average sled dog utilizes oxygen at a rate three times greater than the fittest human. An Olympic marathon runner is almost 1.7 times as efficient in channeling oxygen from the lungs to the cells' metabolic machinery as an average 30-year-old human. A thoroughbred horse is about 3.5 as efficient as the 30-year-old. An average sled dog is about 5.6 times more efficient. They run 10 to 12 hours a day for 10 or 11 days.

Typically, teams run six to eight hours depending on the trail and weather. They cover about 50 to 60 miles. They rest for about six to eight hours, and then do it again.

In a 24-hour period, the musher usually has four to five hours of rest, some of which will be actual sleep. The run-rest cycle reflects Maslow's hierarchy of needs, always balancing fatigue and hunger, never wanting fatigue to take precedence. This way the dogs never get so tired that they will pass up a good meal.

Premium quality, dry food (high calorie density) makes up the meals. Also, lamb, chicken, beef, beaver, or pork is used. Some dogs are given yogurt or cream cheese and other select goodies.

Bozo, one of Frank's dogs, by the time he is 11 years old, pulls him in excess of 30,000 miles, greater than the circumference of the earth. Bozo runs eight Yukon Quests, plus many other races, and he does an Arctic expedition in 2002 of over 1000 miles.

The dogs are capable of going up to 100 miles in 12 hours. They do this on a finishing run from Braeburn to Whitehorse in the Yukon Quest. Every two hours or so, the musher gives the dogs a wet snack for hydration and energy. The exact run-rest cycle is a balancing act informed by the musher's experience.

Strength

Julian, a 200 lb. yellow mastiff, in 1896 ferries load after load to the top of Chilkoot Pass, and on to Lake Bennett pulling more than a thousand pounds over rough ice and into strong winds. He then leads the Berry party down the frozen Yukon River, reaching the mining camp of Forty Mile months before other prospectors who wait for the ice to breakup at Lake Bennett.

Julian breaks the record for pulling the heaviest loads of any dog in the Klondike. London partially models Buck on Julian. A turning point in *The call of the wild* comes when Buck breaks a sled out of the ice weighing a thousand pounds and pulls it for a hundred yards winning a thousand dollars for his master.

Julian is reportedly the model for Buck in Jack London's *The call of the wild.*

The typical dog sled in the Quest weighs between 50 pounds and 180 pounds, without the musher. The weight varies for each leg of the race. In shorter distances, it is less; in longer distances, more. The dogs have to be strong enough to pull a loaded sled up four mountains, often on glare ice against ferocious winds.

Northern dogs

Mushers prefer the Alaskan Huskies because they perform. Breeders develop Alaskan Huskies to either sprint short distances or run moderate speeds for prolonged marathon distances.

The dogs are hybrids: some Siberian, maybe some Labrador, Retriever, or Collie. Over the years, Poodle, Greyhound, and St. Bernard join the gene pool.

The perceived effect of global warming on northern climate influences some mushers to breed dogs with shorter hair, using, for example, German Short-haired Pointers. If the weather gets too cold, insulated coats protect the dogs. More recently some hybrids wear ear muffs, fueling the ongoing debate about what constitutes a northern dog.

Although there is no direct wolf breeding in Alaskan Huskies, all dogs' DNA goes back to the wolf. Being in the team draws on the deep innate desire to be part of the pack. The wolf continues to have an almost mystical or psychic power over domesticated dogs. *The call of the wild* captures the tension between the two worlds.

Roles

Each dog has a precise role. The dog can be a lead, swing, team, or wheel dog.

Frank is alpha

There are no alpha dogs in the team. There is only one alpha—Frank. In the end he is the one who accepts responsibility for what does or does not happen. Frank has no respect for mushers who blame the dogs for things that go wrong.

Mushers should believe in the team. They must build and maintain trust. It is not the dogs' fault if the musher loses faith, or breaks the trust. Mushing necessarily entails a relationship with a team.

If something else is desired, then Frank urges that the person get a snowmobile where the relationship reduces to a mechanical act of pushing a button.

A musher builds the dogs' endurance, strength, speed, and experience with weather and terrain, and, most importantly experience as a high performance team. But, a musher can't teach some things such as finding a trail in a blinding snowstorm. Mushers must be wise and confident enough to trust their dogs.

Lead dog

The lead dog remembers past trails. Often the leader follows current trails even in impossible conditions. The leader is the first to encounter a moose, break through overflow, go over an edge in a wild snowstorm, or accept the musher's commands.

An effective lead dog sets a good pace for the rest of the team, anticipates the challenges ahead, shows confidence of command, and performs at a consistently high level. Conversely, he may be the first to balk at a command because of exhaustion, concern, or confusion.

Like the musher, the lead dog teaches. An experienced lead dog pulls a younger lead dog left when the musher calls "*haw.*" Dogs lead dogs. They know their way around and they motivate the other dogs.

Leaders specialize in different skills. The fast dogs are pace leaders. The musher uses them when speed is needed. Some dogs are needed for strength. They help cross big hills and lead other dogs in situations that require strength.

Other leaders specialize in passing other teams, finding impossible trails, and combating a storm.

Other roles

Swing dogs run behind the lead dogs. They are second in command, the 2IC of the team. They let the leaders lead by keeping the other dogs in line. They stop the team dogs from taking short cuts or drifting sideways. Team dogs pull and maintain a solid pace. They follow the example of the leaders.

The wheel dogs are immediately in front of the sled. They anchor the sled and initially get it moving. This work demands bigger and stronger dogs.

The gender of the dog matters. The males are bigger and stronger. The females are smaller but concentrate more. Just like life in general, squirrels, rabbits, and birds distract the males. In contrast, the females always look down the trail; they focus.

Dogs with attitude

Frank primarily looks for dogs with attitude for his Quest team. He looks for happy dogs that are eager to perform. They have heart. They get up and work even if they don't feel like it.

More than winning Frank wants dogs with attitude crossing the Quest finish line. This means they hold their tails high, pull with a lively gait, and grin as only dogs can.

Task #3 for passionate leaders

Passionate leaders deeply understand what the right jobs are and they find the right people for them. A successful quest demands it.

Right jobs

The wrong person in the wrong job is like Moe, one of the Three Stooges, performing dental surgery. The crippled fit between the right person in the wrong job and the wrong person in the right job wastes energy, time, and money. The mismatch disheartens employees, slows progress, and distracts from goals.

The passionate leader needs to be the custodian of what constitutes the right job, not the HR department, not third party consultants, not individual managers in well-fortified silos.

Anyone in a formal leadership position who does not know what it takes to get the job done should not be in that position. Bravado, temper, or flurries of inappropriate activity often obscure the boss's deficient knowledge of what the right jobs are:

- A newly appointed CEO of a telephone company announces the take over of a car rental company. Nobody sees the connection. His rhetorical flourishes sustain momentum for a short period. In less than a year, the Board of Directors, who know neither the right job nor the right person, give the CEO a golden handshake, and they spin the roulette wheel once again.

- The enrollments stagnate at a mid-sized California university. The Vice President wallows in his ignorance, intolerance, and fears. He does not know what to do. He stifles discussion with threats. His temper shackles the Deans.

- The managing director of a company that supplies pet products forces the senior managers to rehash for the fifth time the perennial product innovation list of impossible dreams. The conversations recycle; the conclusions don't change. Meanwhile, the sales on the West Coast decrease 40%.

For Frank, it would be irresponsible to not know and appreciate what it takes for an epic journey. It would be immoral to take ill-suited dogs on such a trip. In like manner, passionate leaders know and appreciate the crucial components and critical paths of work.

Their ability to successfully lead depends upon it. Lucid knowledge fuels their passion, and that, in turn, sparks others. Their activity is smoothly efficient, sharply focused, and appropriately decisive.

In contrast to ordinary leaders with cloudy visions, passionate leaders communicate not only what the right jobs are, but why. With clear vision, clean execution, and compelling communication, the fire burns brightly.

Right people

Frank does not take an injured, unskilled, or improperly trained dog on a 1000-mile run over mountains in extreme conditions. The dog would end up on the sled, not pulling the weight and burdening other dogs. The long, arduous journey requires super athletes with good attitudes.

Frank puts a strong dog in the lead for the difficult climbs. He puts a speedy dog in for the quick dashes. The right individuals get the right jobs.

He has crystalline clarity about the work that a Quest dog must do to race 1000 miles from the specialty skills of each dog on the team to the support staff along the route. It is a high art for him and a well-developed craft.

At Muktuk, Frank studies the dogs throughout their lives to find the right dogs for the right jobs.

In like manner, when you know the right jobs, spend inordinate time finding the right people who will run the strong race to your "Fairbanks."

Be the custodian

Just as you need to be custodian of what the jobs are, you need to be custodian of who the right people are. **You need people who have fire in their bellies, courage in their voices, and nurturing in their hearts.**

You do not need people who safely and blandly survive a repertoire of overly precise, irrelevant filters from outside companies that don't understand your quest, values, or what constitutes a right job.

Raise the selection process to the same high art that Frank does. The payoff is huge—star employees, inordinate productivity, and dog loyalty. The process itself sends a message.

How many companies run with injured employees? They are burned out, jaded, in chronic pain, or depressed. They are physically or mentally hurt.

How many companies run with unskilled employees who don't have experience, knowledge, or talent to deliver? How many run with employees who are not properly trained or developed?

All of them, . . . all of them end up in the sled. They don't pull their weight and they burden other employees. Just as the dogs know who is in the sled, so do the employees, and they resent it. Furthermore, they resent leaders who don't correct the situation.

The chances for a high performance team increase dramatically when a critical number of right people are in the right jobs. Don't settle for the convenient person. Find the right person.

Find employees who don't ride in the sled, but eagerly run and pull in front of it. Find people who give energy rather than drain it. Find individuals who stimulate, create, perpetually learn, and leap into the air with a love of life.

Just as the dogs have attitude, the people who surround you should have attitude that optimizes interaction, productivity, and conviviality. They too should hold their metaphoric tails high, pull with a lively gait, and grin as dogs do.

For your quest and values, there is no more important task than getting the right people into the right jobs.

In your personal life, your quest may not be business oriented. The principle is the same, however. **See every person as a source of learning.**

The person may be smarter, wiser, older, or more experienced. Or, the person may be a special challenge, a child with a disability, a gifted athlete, or an 18-year-old son trying to discover his life's course. When you find right person, the potential to teach you becomes the right job. The learning will fuel your passion.

chapter four

Obtain permission to lead!

When leaders know they have permission to lead, they do not depend upon threat or reward to control followers. Even though they may be in a position of authority, they influence others through trust.

My wife abhors being controlled. For this reason, she cannot get into swing dance lessons, where the man leads and the female follows. The breakthrough comes when a female instructor says, *"You must give him permission to lead."* The dogs are the same. They give the musher permission to lead.

Mushers cannot physically control the collective energy of 14 dogs that are strong enough to drag a dozen handlers behind a sled. They only control them through the relationship.

In essence, a dog team is about relationships. The dogs are not machines. A machine doesn't care who turns the key; the dogs do. Consequently, the puzzle, mystery, and challenge is to understand each dog individually and then build from the chemistry.

Frank crafts 14 moving puzzles into one dynamic dog team ready to race in an extreme event with an extraordinary number of variables. Just the combinations of placing the dogs on a tow line are huge—over 87 billion unique possibilities.

In the Quest, where survival depends upon high performance and mutual trust, the quality of the relationship determines the behaviors and attitudes. Trust is the foundation of everything.

Dogs work for owners—that's their nature. But loyalty and performance depend not on ownership, but reciprocated trust and mutual stewardship. Only Buck's last master, John Thornton, in *The call of the wild* wins his loyalty:

> Such was the communion in which they lived, the strength of Buck's gaze would draw John Thornton's head around, and he would return the gaze, without speech, his heart shining out of his eyes as Buck's heart shone out. (Jack London, *The call of the wild*)

Reciprocated trust

Reciprocated trust creates a synergistic relationship. If the musher compromises or breaks the relationship, the dogs slow down or stop. Frank monitors nuances in behavior, and so do the dogs.

Snow blind trust

During the first Quest in 1984, the biting cold, ranting and raving wind, and abrasive snow force five teams to lash themselves together on the leeward side of Eagle Summit.

The ice builds up on the dogs' eyelashes and freezes them shut. It blinds Daryle Adkins's lead dogs. Their instincts tell them to turn their backs to the wind and huddle down.

However, when Daryle coaxes his blinded dogs forward, they override their instincts, in effect, giving him permission to lead them. This unwavering trust in Daryle allows five teams to make it across the hardest part of the mountain.

Stretched trust

When Frank and his team climb the 200-meter, 30-degree slope at Eagle Summit in the 2001 Quest, the dogs go faster than he does. It is the Heartbreak Hill of the race.

He jumps on the back of the sled because he is tired. At this point the dogs stop. Frank does not have permission to ride in the toughest part of their struggle. This is not part of the deal. They look at him with what Frank describes as disgust. Amazing.

When Frank sees their expressions, he either projects his own sense of inadequacy or he accurately reads the dogs' emotions.

If it is a projection, Sophocles (497-406/5 B.C.) must be whispering in his ear: *All is disgust when a man leaves his own nature and does what is unfit.* Frank thinks that the dogs think he has done something unfit.

If it is not a projection, but a reaction to the dogs' real emotions, then Frank must respond. Either interpretation has consequences for the relationship that is now bruised and perhaps injured.

Frank gets off the sled and edges past it. The dogs wait on the slope and watch every step. When he gets a little way above the sled, he gives two short whistles. He has no doubt that the dogs will come—no doubt. And, they do.

He repeats this process three times before the team makes it over the summit. His trust and their loyalty take them up and over the top. The relationship is everything.

Later, another musher tells him that if he had the slightest doubt, the dogs would not have come.

Broken trust

Sometimes the dogs deny permission. At the same spot in 1995, Larry "Cowboy" Smith leads the rest of the Quest field handily. When he gets over the summit, he can coast to an easy win.

But Larry violates the trust. He drives his dogs too hard attending to his needs, not their needs. His dogs decide that they have had enough. They lie down and refuse to go on.

After the dogs rest sufficiently, they acquiesce to the relationship again. Larry is now in fourth place, nine hours behind Frank who wins the Quest with the fastest time ever, and with happy dogs.

Mutual stewardship

The musher-dog relationship transcends a master-servant association where pragmatic factors such as financial need, obligations, or contracts bind. The highest bidder controls these fickle bonds.

When the financial tie stops, the servant disappears. Financial freedom breaks the bond. No love is lost. None existed in the first place.

Mutual and intense loyalty bind the relationship. Just as the musher is steward of his dogs, his dogs are stewards of him. The north abounds with stories of reciprocal love.

Frank's stewardship

The Quest race itself reflects most dramatically Frank's stewardship. After each run sequence, Frank immediately attends to the dogs. He gets the ice out of their paws. Sometimes the dogs return the favor by biting ice from Frank's beard.

He heats water and prepares food. In some instances, a dog won't eat what's on the menu. Frank accommodates the dog, offering other food. He readies a bed of straw and perhaps a foam mat.

He checks their feet frequently, even though his hands are cold and numb. Over the ten or eleven day race, Frank changes 1000 to 1200 booties.

He watches the dogs' weight and pays close attention to their attitudes. He knows each idiosyncratic mood. He massages their sore muscles, and he talks to them. Then, and only then, he attends to his needs. *How many managers attend this carefully to their employees?*

Mouth to mouth rescue

In 1987, Jeff King breaks trail in front of his dogs. He does not realize that a towline wraps around a dog's neck and strangles him.

Rick Atkinson, another Quest competitor, pulls the lifeless dog from the snow. He repeatedly gives the dog mouth-to-mouth resuscitation. He saves the dog.

It does not bother him that the revived dog finishes the race in third place with Jeff's team. Rick finishes in fifth place. The other mushers name him as most deserving of the 1987 Sportsman Trophy.

Baldy of Nome

Baldy, the lead dog for Scotty Allen, moves to legendary status during Nome's Solomon Derby, one of the earliest dogsled races (1910) in Alaska. At the halfway point near Solomon, Baldy no longer hears the soothing sound of his musher's voice.

Baldy saves his musher and wins the race. He becomes the subject of a book.

Baldy stops the team and turns them around. He finds the unconscious Scotty lying on the trail bleeding from the head. An iron trail marker had knocked him off the sled when he leaned down to adjust the brake.

Baldy wakes the musher and drags him into the basket on the sled. They win the 65-mile race and claim the Derby prize. Later, Esther Birdsall immortalizes Baldy in 1913 in a book called *Baldy of Nome*.

Iditarod champion

One hundred years later, Susan Butcher, four-time Iditarod champion, breaks through ice and falls into icy water. She loses her breath and can't talk. She thinks she is going under, but her two lead dogs immediately pull her out.

In the near tragedies for Scott and Susan, the dogs care for and protect their musher. Both human and dog devote themselves to each other. Both choose a relationship that goes beyond simple stimulus-response reactions.

Shared learning

Just as the musher teaches the dogs, the dogs teach the musher. After 11 years of competing, the dogs teach Frank how to win in the 1995 Quest. The lesson is a Zen paradox. They teach Frank that he can drive them by letting them go. *"That insight has implanted itself forever on my brain,"* says Frank.

Connecting with energy

Frank consciously connects with both the physical and psychological energy that the dogsled team generates. He channels it so that it gets them down the trail as fast and smoothly as possible.

He recalls the year that he has a team that most people think very capable of winning the race. The dogs are so powerful that Frank fails to connect with their full energy. During the race, he spends much of his time trying to hold them back. They relentlessly drag him. He resists their power, almost to the point that it is comical.

During this race, Frank is not on the same page as the dogs. By the time he lets them go, there is too much lost ground to make up. They finish the race in the top five, but he knows that he has failed the team. The lesson uses a principle of judo: **Use the energy by not resisting it**.

Performance

Every time Frank takes a team out to train them, he never asks for 110%. That request makes little sense to him. It is presumptuous and insulting. There is no 110%. He sees that as a myth.

He trains them incrementally. He moves them, say from 75% to 80% performance. If they are 80% right, he doesn't get hung up on the last 20% looking for perfection. At the same time, even small improvements are important. He never asks them for more than they can do. He knows precisely where his dogs are and how much to push them.

Like a parent and child, reciprocated trust and mutual stewardship do not preclude somebody from being top dog, especially if permission is granted.

Occasionally, he disciplines the same way a female dog controls her young, by biting the dog's ear. It is a painful, but not injurious bite, and usually occurs on training runs. By doing this, Frank reaffirms his "top dog" status. The bite is powerfully symbolic.

There is a moment in *The call of the wild* where Buck returns the musher's love with a feigned bite:

> Buck had a trick of love expression that was akin to hurt. He would often seize Thornton's hand in his mouth and close so fiercely that the flesh bore the impress of his teeth for some time afterward. (Jack London, *The call of the wild*)

The contrary messages, a bite but not a bite, affirm a bond of trust. Each is vulnerable to the other, but neither violates the relationship.

Frank sees dual forces defining the dog's identity — the domestic and the primitive. He considers both parts in relating to the dog. It is easier to influence the domestic side and almost impossible to control the primitive side. When a dog fights, for instance, the primitive dominates. When the fight is over, the dog inevitably looks at you with the expression *"The devil made me do it!"*

The team has to pull together. In the end, functioning as a team is more important than pure ability. Five Michael Jordans on the same team don't necessarily create a working team.

Love and discipline go hand in hand for Frank. His survival and the dogs' survival depend on it. He protects them, manages them when in heat, and intervenes when they fight.

Musher leads

If a hazardous condition, a moose, or thin ice jeopardizes their safety, he takes the dogs off the trail even though they prefer to stay on the trail. Sometimes he must get them back onto the trail even though the conditions seem impossible.

One time, the team accidentally gets into a dangerous situation when it misses a trail marker and winds up on a trail heading into a mineshaft. The icy trail freaks the dogs out. Frank exerts his top dog status to stop the dogs in a perilous situation and turn them around.

Also, the musher must be assertive when dogs are in heat. A lovesick dog often pines for a female and stops eating.

David Sawatzky, a Quest musher, ends up with four dogs in heat in the 1993 Quest race. He becomes the interfering parent who dampens true love. He manages to keep them from mating.

But Bruce Milne, a musher from Two Rivers, Alaska, isn't so lucky. It takes him 24 hours to cover 36 miles because a female is in heat. The team travels 1.5 miles per hour instead of the 10 to 14 miles per hour. The mating process, excluding foreplay, takes 20 to 60 minutes.

Dog leads

Driving the dogs is usually straightforward, but occasionally the musher wants to do one thing and the dogs want to do another. For example, if a storm buries a trail, Frank might think it goes right, but his veteran leaders pull left. He knows that his intuition is not perfect. He goes left. Experience and trust prevail.

Frank yields to the dogs. It means giving up the "I know best" or "I am smarter" and trusting that they have better senses and instincts working for them.

In 1925, twenty dog teams contribute to the effort to deliver 300,000 units of serum to Nome, Alaska, a diphtheria-stricken town. Gunner Kaasen runs the last leg of the 600 mile rescue. Winds blow like a hurricane and the temperature drops below -50° F.

Balto, the lead dog, saves the team when, despite Gunner's exhortations, he refuses to go forward. He senses open water underneath a thin layer of snow.

Withdrawing from the race

Withdrawing from the Quest after a year of preparation tests the musher's reciprocated trust and mutual stewardship. He must put the relationship ahead of personal ambition or glory. The iron will must listen to the heart, not the ego. It is a painful and disappointing decision. Frank faces this decision four times over 22 Quests.

Balto and Gunner ran the last leg in the Nome run.

He describes the first time he withdraws. It is 1986, the year of the hardest Quest ever. Frank drifts back in telling the story. He looks at his stubby, sandpaper hands, palms down. His hands shake and his face looks ashen. He relives the memory.

He loses the trail in unrelenting wind and darkness in mountains above 101 Lodge, 416 miles from Dawson City. He and his team crash through snow to the bottom of a steep incline.

Quest dogs
Muktuk Class of 2005

Muktuk dogs at play (Color plate 17).

Beethoven, Carter, Decaf, Falcon, Shilo, Kirby, Livingston, Mischief, Pelly, Sakura, Shubert, Flint, Sprocket, and Stanley on the following pages are Frank's 2005 Yukon Quest team (Color plates 18 through 31)

Beethoven
3 years, 64 pounds, rookie

Beethoven is Schubert's brother, and runs on lead. He is a really good trotter with a super attitude. This is the first Quest for both Schubert and Beethoven.

Carter
3 years, 65 pounds, rookie

Carter is a brother to Beethoven and Schubert. Like them, he is a very steady member of the team. He is one of the few dogs who does not run on lead. This is his first Quest.

Decaf

8 years, 73 pounds,
6 Quests

Decaf is strong, steady, reliable, and good-natured. He has been a leader in Frank's Quest teams since 2000. When he was a puppy, we all thought he would be too big for the Quest, but he has more than proved us wrong. He has the heart of a Quest dog.

Falcon

2.5 years, 66 pounds, rookie

Falcon is a really tall young dog, and he has great spirit. He has the best howl in the yard, and a very handsome face. Falcon is Mischief's brother.

Shilo

6 years, 53 pounds, 1 Quest

The smallest member of our team, Shilo is a sweet, gentle girl. But, she's also a focused and strong leader. More than once, she has pulled bigger, stronger males onto the right trail, and she won't take any nonsense from the boys. Her first Quest was in 2004 where she performed like a professional.

Kirby

8 years, 63 pounds, 5 Quests

Kirby is a big, strong fellow. He is long-legged and a littermate to Terror. He's good tempered and a steady worker. And, as you can see, he's a very handsome fellow.

Livingston

6 years, 63 pounds, 2 Quests

A brother to Stanley, Livingston is a very reliable leader. He is athletic and a bit of a jumper with a tendency to leap four to five feet in the air. When he is not jumping, he is proving himself a great leader in tough conditions, notably on ice.

Mischief

4 years, 60 pounds, 1 Quest

Mischief was the baby of the team last year. He is a goofy dog, determined to live up to his name. Even though he is still young, he is already running on lead.

Pelly

7 years, 71 pounds, 3 Quests

This little sweetie really takes after his mum, Tatchun. He's quiet and hardworking, with a very gentle temperament. On his first Quest, he was very tired by Dawson, but he kept on eating and drinking and working.

Sakura

3 years, 54 pounds, rookie

Sakura is a great little leader, although still a bit tentative at times. She is renowned for jumping over the gangline while waiting to hit the trail. No one has a vertical leap like Sakura!

Schubert

3 years, 65 pounds, rookie

Like most of the dogs, Schubert runs on lead. He is becoming a very steady team member with great attitude.

Flint

4 years, 68 pounds, 2 Quests

Flint was the baby on the team two years ago, and he came through with flying colors. He's gorgeous, and so affectionate that everyone falls in love instantly. He did extremely well as a rookie, and has really matured as a leader. Now, he is a steady member of the team.

Sprocket

3 years, 53 pounds, rookie

Sprocket is a very happy little leader, who just loves getting out there. She had surgery to remove part of her jaw, but the only problematic result has been that she is a slow eater. And she still loves to run!

Stanley

6 years, 63 pounds, 2 Quests

Stanley is relatively new to the Quest trail, but he is turning out to be a fine leader and has shown that he can handle really tough, poorly marked trail conditions.

He turns his dogs loose to dig themselves beds in the snow. He sits down behind his sled to protect himself from the wind.

Daylight reorients Frank and the team. They head to Dawson City, but not before a bizarre event. He and Ron Rosser, another Quest musher, stop at a cabin on the Yukon River not far from Eagle. They are tired and cold. The storm remains ugly.

Darryl, a giant of a man, makes them hot chocolate and talks to them. He is like the kind Dr Jeckle. When they go to leave after warming up for two hours, Darryl advises them to stay because of the storm.

Frank and Ron ignore the advice and set out. Within 200 meters, the storm forces them back to the cabin. This time, Mr. Hyde answers the door. Darryl won't let them in. His rage seems worse than the storm. He forces them to continue. By the time Frank gets to Dawson City, he is numb.

The challenge of the Quest pulls at him to stay in the race even though he has deteriorated badly. He knows that he is now the weakest link in the chain. He consults with a friend.

His friend reminds him to check his ego. Frank scratches to protect himself and his dogs. The stewardship is stronger than the need to compete.

The musher succeeds because he treats his team with an optimal mixture of discipline and love. He knows when, how, and why to be tough. He also knows when, how, and why to show love. He gets the most out of his team when he appropriately balances the two.

Task #4 for passionate leaders

The fourth task for passionate leaders is to obtain permission to lead.

Frank does not ask permission to lead literally, but his ongoing behavior asks. In adverse conditions, dogs know whether they are being forced or asked to work harder. His dogs grant him permission to lead even in difficult situations. **Mutual stewardship brings trust and loyalty.**

In like manner, partners, friends, and employees know whether they are forced or asked. A command sounds different to a request or a favor. A kiss given is different from a kiss stolen.

When you communicate in a dominating way, others perceive that you are controlling. You make them objects of communication. When you communicate in an equitable way, you make them the subject of communication. It is the difference between being acted upon and being invited to act with.

In the work situation, employees strongly sense what constitutes a day's work for a day's pay. Cynically translated, it means they put in the minimal effort for what is required and the company pays the lowest compensation that it can get away with.

Cynicism aside, some employees work minimally and others put in extra effort. Those who value the relationship grant permission to lead, and they run the race harder.

Power of permission

A passionate leader communicates that a person is being asked rather than forced. This message does not let the leader hide behind the barrier of distance. It reduces alienation and sanitization; it promotes authenticity and sincerity.

Employees become "subjects" not "objects" of communication. They become partners in dialogue, not targets of monologue.

The message cultivates trust and respect. It also reflects the confidence of the one seeking permission. It indicates that the person is open, approachable, and sensitive to what it means to ask.

On the ground

Frank monitors his dogs exquisitely. In contrast, poor managers fail to notice their employees' needs, strengths, weaknesses, hopes, and concerns. They talk at them from a position of command and control, not to them as a steward.

They do not get down on the ground with their employees. Metaphorically they do not get the ice out of their paws. One of the most powerful images of the *Bible* occurs when Christ gets down on the ground and washes the feet of his disciples.

Expectations

Permission to lead does not give leadership away. It still entails tough love. When the other person grants permission, they expect that the leader will hold individuals accountable.

Passionate leaders do not ignore or reward bad behavior. They do not tolerate mediocre performances. They recognize exceptional work and celebrate it.

On the other hand, when people perceive a boss-employee relationship rather than a stewardship model, the *quid pro quo* model of a pragmatic day's wage for a pragmatic day's work drives them.

Furthermore, they control what constitutes a day's work. They will not put in significantly more hours simply because they are exhorted, ordered to, or urged to. They are not crazy.

The power of permission means that the employee is more likely to have buy-in, that is, the person understands, believes, and accepts what the company is trying to do.

Individuals become active agents when they grant permission. They become a party in a relationship. When individuals grant permission, they tacitly establish a contract with the other.

Passionate leaders gain partnerships that lead to reciprocated trust, mutual stewardship, and shared learning. It no longer is a one way street. Both parties work to exceed expectations.

When this happens, you have one of the necessary conditions in place for a fantastic run.

chapter five

Develop an iron will!

Passionate leaders have an iron will. They do what they say they are going to do. Unwavering focus eliminates distractions. Their execution does not tolerate procrastination, inefficiency, or poor working relations. Like the gold rushers, their resolve drives them forward. Sometimes the will breaks.

Chilkoot Pass in the winter, and the requirements to bring 2000 pounds of supplies to survive a year in the Yukon, stop many gold rush dreamers. They turn around and head back down the Inner Passage, on the ships they came in. They do not have the iron will that takes over 30,000 dreamers, up the mountain, over Chilkoot Pass, and down the Yukon River.

Initially, many stampeders do not have sufficient knowledge of the new territory. But the Yukon quickly hardens them. They learn to construct a boat, run the treacherous rapids of the Yukon River, kill game, build a cabin, drive dogs or horses, prospect, and mine land. The Yukon is kinder to those who have both the will and skill.

In the early days, the mushers and their dogs not only work hard, but play hard. The mushers from Yukon River villages drive their dogs up to 500 miles just to get to a dogsled race.

Iron will

Today, the Quest musher shows the same physical and mental discipline of the early gold rushers. At every turn, forces test the will.

William Kleedehn, who has an artificial leg, personifies an iron will. He whimsically names his kennel "Limp-a-long."

Personal discipline

Self-doubt, sickness, and death temper the mushers' wills. In 1995, Frank wins the Yukon Quest in the fastest time ever. He wins the race in ten days, 16 hours, and 20 minutes. However, he wrestles with memories coming into the race.

A drug penalty for inadvertently giving his dogs Ibuprofen bruises his reputation. The top competitors dismiss him as a real threat because he has never been in the top prize money, winning only an average of $1018 over eleven Quests. Scratching the year before reminds him of his physical vulnerabilities.

And, the death of his friend and fellow musher, Bruce Johnson, the year before preoccupies him. Nevertheless, Frank overcomes these adversities with determination and unwavering focus.

After his unprecedented win in the 1995 Yukon Quest, his understanding of what it means to be a passionate leader crystallizes.

Three principles ingrain themselves in him. First, he **believes in himself**. He refuses to focus on doubting. Second, he **does not underestimate** anyone and he does not underestimate himself. Third, he resolutely **believes in his team,** even though it takes tough mental discipline to hold on to this concept.

Bruce Lee

Bruce Lee, winner of the 1999 Quest, exemplifies the combination of will and skill that makes a difference. It is the tenth day of the Quest. John Balzer in *Yukon Alone* immortalizes the story.

Bruce is in Central, the last checkpoint before the notorious Eagle Summit. Winds and blowing snow reduce visibility to zero. Coincidently, parts of the slope are as steep as the Golden Steps up Chilkoot Pass that the stampeders climbed.

At ten minutes to noon, Bruce heads to Eagle Summit, 33 miles away. The first 13 miles are easy, but then the trail gets steeper and the wind fiercer. Bruce cannot see his lead dogs and he cannot see trail markers.

He trusts his dogs to stay on the trail away from the edge. He feels the sled level out. They are at the bottom of the mountain's headwall right before two extremely steep slopes separated by a gentle transition slope.

The dogs slip on glaze ice. Gales whip down the slope to counter lunging efforts. The dogs claw several hundred feet and then stop.

Bruce crawls up the towline to reassure the team. He pushes the sled and shouts for the dogs to go. Nothing. He changes leaders and tries again. They stop after ten feet. He changes leaders again. Nothing. The dogs lie down in the snow and turn their heads away from the wind.

He pushes the sled forward until it hits his wheel dogs. Then he crawls forward and hoists his lead dog to its feet and pulls. He gains eight feet. He repeats this process three more times to gain 24 feet. Then the steepness of the slope stops him.

He unloads the sled, and then repeats the push-pull process again, and again, and again. Then he anchors the sled and relays the food and gear up the hill, 120 feet at a time.

He repeats the whole process. He tips the sled to one runner and wiggles it to stop a backward slide. He gains eight feet and eight feet and eight more agonizing feet.

The ground levels finally. He is on the transition slope. Miraculously the weather lifts. The sun shines. He relays the food and gear up to the more level slope and repacks the sled.

When he gives the word to start, the dogs don't head up the trail, but turn and head down. He stops the sled, unpacks it, and begins the push-pull process to win incremental gains.

Now he makes a mistake. He strips off his sweat drenched parka and fleece layer underneath. He works faster and harder to stay warm. His sweat begins to freeze when he stops.

He checks his team. He sees something in Clovis, the last dog he picked for the team, which he had not seen before. Instinctively he moves Clovis to lead position. He taps the handlebar on the sled and the dogs go forward. They pass the gear, food, and the parka. They claw and lunge and stumble their way against the wind up the second steep slope.

The steepness exhausts Bruce two-thirds up the slope. He stops. He talks to his dogs. He tells them that they need to get him and them through it . . . that they can't stop. Each dog listens, and then they turn and climb the remaining third to the top.

Even though they conquer the top, Bruce is in serious trouble. The wind punches him around, upsets his balance. The dropping temperature begins freezing parts of his body, the extremities first. The lurking darkness threatens to raise the stakes further.

He has minutes to get back down to his parka and other clothes or die. The wind lowers the chill factor to minus 70. The bone chilling cold numbs his hands and threatens the fingers in particular. He is scared.

He makes it to his clothes and clumsily puts on every layer. He windmills his arms to reclaim his hands. He trots in circles to build up body heat and circulation. Eventually, he feels the fiery throb of blood in his hands, pain and joy at the same time.

He carries all his food and gear back up the ice chute, load by load, packs the sled and gives word to his dogs. They bolt down the trail heading for the Taj Mahal, in reality, a ten-by-twenty foot shack at Mile 101 checkpoint.

Bruce wins the 1999 Quest with a time of eleven days, eleven hours, and twenty-seven minutes.

His experience from five Quests, and his knowledge of the mountain, especially the Eagle Summit trail, get his dogs through to a critical point. The team's relationship with Bruce, in turn, gets him through.

Discipline

Many demons stalk the Quest. A musher draws strength to fight them from a life orientation that fits comfortably and gives an inner peace.

Balanced life style

The mushers sacrifice many things long before the race. Some give up the company of fellow human beings and live with their dogs. They forgo normal amenities of home, isolate themselves from the social comfort of community, and compromise relationships to focus on the dogs.

Frank has grown to another level. It no longer is an "either-or" for him; it is a hearty and healthy "both-and."

I ask Frank what would be his decision if he had to choose between Anne, his partner, and the dogs, the type of decision he had to make earlier in his life. He looks befuddled. He can't process the question; it makes no sense.

He cannot separate the magic woman who let him into her life, the dogs who shape his identity, his extended family, and his northern community. The gestalt is everything. It motivates and satisfies. Frank is at peace with himself.

Demons

Sleep deprivation, distractions, and an avalanche of details test the musher's mental discipline. Each demon picks at him in different ways.

Some strike early and only reveal their consequences late in the race. An overlooked detail hurts Frank in the 1997 Quest. He can't change the runners on his sled easily because the screwdriver is the wrong type.

It takes him over an hour to complete what should have been a five-minute task. He places second in the race 68 minutes behind Rick Mackey.

Some demons team up and accumulate their impact. Hunger, dehydration, and lack of sleep conjure illusions so real, so appropriate that the musher cannot separate the real from the non-real, the perfect illustration of "Maya," the Hindu concept of the real-and-not-real at the same time. It stops the person's world.

Headlamps dance in the sky. Voices call from the woods. Trees come alive and march along the river. A bear attacks. Spears and swords fly through the air. Family and friends magically join the team. Dogs mysteriously run down the trail backwards and disappear in black holes. Alice-in-Wonderland reality creeps in. Salvador Dali landscapes suddenly make sense. All are hallucinations. Each one is a crack in the iron will.

Some demons shun the subtle and strike swiftly and without warning. Overflow ice breaks. Tons of snow let go of the mountain. A storm lures the musher out of the sunshine then surrounds him with white fury. And, in the most devastating situation, a dog unpredictably dies.

Some demons haunt the musher for the whole race: missed trails, poor organization, and badly timed rest-run schedules.

After 22 Quests, Frank knows how to tame many of the demons. He fights boredom with memories of 22 Quests, songs from the 60s and 70s, and conversations, like aged wine play in his head.

His audio senses dominate. He remembers one-hit wonders like *The Girl from Ipanema* and *Wooly Bully*. He hears Chubby Checker's *Twist* and Little Eva's *Loco-Motion*. He recalls *The Leader of the Pack* and *Ode to Billy Joe*. *Johnny B. Goode*, *Born To Be Wild*, and *I'm a Believer* pop up anytime.

Accomplished skill

All the will in the world won't get a musher through, if he doesn't have the skill. Jack London parodies a willful set of mushers in *The call of the wild:*

> They did not know how to do anything, and as the days went by it became apparent that they could not learn. They were slack in all things, without order or discipline. It took them half the night to pitch a slovenly camp, and half the morning to break that camp and get the sled loaded in fashion so slovenly that the rest of the day they were occupied in stopping and re-arranging the load. (Jack London, *The call of the wild*)

In contrast, Frank in partnership with Anne epitomizes organization. She runs the mandatory 36-hour Dawson stop with the military precision of Major Margaret Houlihan in *M*A*S*H*.

She gives each handler a binder detailing minute-by-minute responsibilities. Nobody wants Anne to bite their ear. His support team sets a high standard for dogs and human care.

Frank's detailed training and northern knowledge protect him from many surprises.

Self training

To work with his team, he starts with himself. He looks at his own strengths and limitations. If he doesn't honestly assess himself, others will not take him seriously. As the Quest approaches, he increases his own training.

He must be fit enough to run and climb with the dogs over the 1000-mile course, pack and unpack the sled, and serve 14 dogs efficiently and tirelessly. A strong back, powerful arms and legs, a well-conditioned heart and cardiovascular system are entry stakes.

Mushers must understand physical processes. A cold, dry day, for instance, increases sweat and breathing, which dehydrates the person.

Dogs' training

Frank works with twenty dogs in preparation for the Quest. Each day he puts them in situations where they can learn, where they can try a new trail, hill, or stretch of ice.

The most critical element in training is being consistent. He establishes clear training objectives. Deviation from the objectives wastes time and resources.

He loves the training sessions. New trails and unique weather neither distract nor surprise, but challenge him to solve riddles, sometimes instantly. *"Quick, what is the sound of one hand clapping?" "Quick, why is the ice so soft?" "Quick, why did the dogs balk?"*

The gait of each dog talks to him. The color of the day, it doesn't matter if it is gray, energizes him. The dogs play a symphony for him with their rhythm, pace, quick glances, and even answering the call of nature. Information fills his attention about the dog's ability to recover, its mental attitude, and responsiveness.

Frank crafts the moments of receptivity on the training runs by talking to the team only when it is needed. When he does speak, the team knows it is important.

He intermittently talks to individual dogs, always saying their name first. "*Herschel, good dog. Good dog, Herschel.*" The praise sounds like praise should. "*Terror, gee, gee. Terror, good boy.*" The instructions sound like instructions should. "*Stanley* (prolonging his name so that he knows to stop doing what he was doing)." The reminder sounds like a reminder should.

Frank, similar to the miner finding gold in the land, or Jack London finding gold in the stories, finds a rich vein in each day's learning.

Early in the season, Frank uses resistance training to build the dogs' muscles. He optimizes the muscles for each dog, being careful not to build too much mass which changes the dog's gait, reach, or drive.

Frank builds the dogs' cardiovascular system through long-slow-distance training. As the Quest gets nearer, he begins advanced training. He runs the dogs at or near peak performance. He alternates between fast and slow runs.

He appraises the performance of all the dogs. His goal is to develop them to be the best possible sled dogs they can be. In turn, he judges himself on how successful he has been in supporting them to achieve their potential.

Northern knowledge

Northern knowledge about terrain, weather, ice, and water serves Frank well, and he generously shares what he knows.

Frank's website describes the trail from point to point.

Most northerners pay more attention to the weather than the news. The musher reads the wind and snow, light and color, and temperature. He understands deep cold that penetrates the bones so much that hot food and fire do not relieve the pain.

He balances between being too cold and too hot for both him and his dogs. For this reason, the musher often runs through the night, before the day heats the temperature up another 10 degrees.

At breakfast one morning in October, Frank jumps up and shouts, *"There's ice on the river."* He marks the calendar. The white chunks of ice flowing on the Takhini River enhance moods like an euphoric drug.

Frank watches how the river freezes. He notes when the ice gets thick enough and where changing surface pressures can trap a dog. Ice masks danger in different ways. Thin ice scares the musher.

Conditions under any ice can change within four or five hours. To fall into water and not recover means death. In subzero cold, a wet musher has minutes to get out of his wet clothes and dry out.

Stationary fog on the river signals a probable open spot in the ice. He listens for river currents at night, another signal that a hazard may lurk. He watches for a hundred and one other traps, many disguised. And, he trusts that his dogs sense dangers beyond his ability to detect them.

Experience

Frank remembers scenarios from 22 Quests. He knows the strengths of the hardened Quest competitors. He knows the weaknesses of the rookies and what would help them. He does not panic because a new musher seems to have an insurmountable lead.

The northern lights smile upon him, as do First Nation elders, family, and friends from around the world. The Quest gives him the appreciation that he needs.

The Quest honors the people who settle the northern territory, and they, in turn, inspire the mushers and everyone else associated with the race.

The northerners celebrate the last place finisher as much as the first place finisher. Symbolically, he or she gets a red lantern, the light at the end of the train to signal that all are home safely. Barry Emmett has half dozen red lanterns from various dogsled events. In 1994 he takes 16 days to earn the lantern. Even the last place finishers demonstrate the prerequisite will and skill to survive the toughest dogsled race in the world.

Task #5 for passionate leaders

Passionate leaders have the musher's iron will to complete a quest. They focus unwaveringly on what has to be done.

Stagnation, laziness, and procrastination symptomatically reveal lack of will. The person who whimsically attends to anything, endlessly misanalyzes, inappropriately prioritizes, or fears success shows lack of will. The boss who tolerates mediocrity, bullying in the workplace, and long term inefficiencies shows lack of will.

Zombies

Typically, I ask CEOs the following question: "Are there any zombies in your organization?" One CEO from a regional clothing manufacturer says, *"Yes, half the company is in zombie mode."* I don't have to say what a zombie is. She tells me.

"People come to work at eight in the morning, check in their brains and then come alive at five in the afternoon when they go home."

I ask her what it costs the company to be in zombie mode half the time. She has no idea. It does not show up on the accountant's books. It won't be part of the profit-loss statement. I ask how long have they been in zombie mode. With a straight face she says, *"About nine years, ever since I've been here."*

The zombie maker is the problem, not the workers. She lacks the will to track zombie losses, and the skill to revitalize a sleeping work force. The primary intervention needs to be for the zombie maker. A program to fix the workers while leaving the zombie maker in tact exacerbates the problem.

Curious appearance of iron will

In this example, the owner of a company that makes children's furniture is comfortably happy with his situation. At the annual senior management retreat, he declares an ambitious $130 million dollar sales goal.

Six senior managers study the goal with arched eyebrows, jaded indifference, and bored resignation. Nobody challenges him. Nobody believes the goal, but everybody nods agreement and appears to sign on. Their passive sabotage will be invisible. The CEO is happy.

However, I challenge an owner's thinking. In light of their nonchalance, I propose that he issue a million dollar challenge to his indifferent managers.

First, he will write each senior manager a check for $1,000,000 at the end of the fiscal year if they achieve $160 million in sales. Second, they must do it without his leadership.

All of a sudden, iron will curiously appears. Almost immediately the managers unanimously agree that it can be done. Then they begin to discuss how.

Their respective silos disappear. They no longer protect their territory. They are animated and dramatic. They critically evaluate each other's areas with no defensiveness.

At the end of the exercise, they are confident that they can do it and agree to monitor and hold each other accountable. They readily dump some of the CEO's personal projects, one of which he likes because it is the first product he sold when he started. Now it loses $100,000 each year.

For the next year, they promise to frequently monitor and help each other. They expect that the meetings will be radically different, no distractions, priority focusing, and geared to the quest. They will drive values, not the owner.

It sounds like money motivates them, but it is more complicated than that. The incentive shifts perceived recognition and reward, and the magnitude of the incentive offers managers increased freedom.

"I will do it!"

Where does the leader get iron will? Where does the resolve come from? Who grants it? Who crafts it? You do!

You are the will maker. You ultimately say, *"I will do it."* To get to the *"I will do it"* you need to know what you want to get to, and you need to know whether you are prepared to put in the effort. Your quest and values loom largely in the decision.

Once you say *"I will do it"* then discipline and execution become the taskmasters. If your quest is worthy, the journey rewards you for your work, pain, and sacrifices more than you imagine. You can do it!

chapter six

Foster community support!

Passionate leaders do not passively live and work in communities. Instead, they foster communities that stimulate them. Being an active agent in a community results in support, love, and reassurance. Giving to a community triggers a chain reaction that inevitably gives back in kind. Energy begets energy.

Macrocosm

When the *Seattle Post-Intelligencer* announces the Klondike gold discovery, a macrocosm of dreamers descends on Dawson City. The dreamers who come to the Yukon are restless. Comfort, contentment, safety, a guaranteed job, or the "known" is not strong enough to hold them in their job or situation.

The dreamers are ambitious, possibly irrational, maybe greedy, some desperate, but all certainly hopeful. The gold rush compounded by a lingering economic depression in the U.S. attracts all trades, all ages, and all ambitions. It promises a new beginning and a new life.

A harsh, wintry, exquisitely beautiful environment takes them by the throat and shakes them around until they change and change again.

Day-to-day, season-to-season survival molds the early settlers. They still dream, but the edge is harder, more pragmatic. They see themselves as both romantic and realistic. They are tolerant of a spectrum of characters ranging from the invisible worker to the outrageously colorful characters like Arizona Charlie Meadows, Circle City Mickey, Dog Salmon Bob, Silent Sam Bonnifield, Nelly the Pig, Limejuice Lil, and Evaporated Kid.

The settlers are stubborn and self-reliant, but at the same time depend on a wide-ranging community that extends beyond any tiny town.

Early communities

The first prospectors allow other miners who don't strike pay dirt to go onto their claims to take enough gold to outfit themselves for the next season. The act is not charity but an investment in dignity and pride. The golden rule prevails but is not flaunted.

A man's word gets him credit, and that word is seldom broken. The old-timer never speculates in food. He lets his neighbor have flour at the price it costs him in the store.

The miners survive by their wits. They make do, innovate, and invent.

After the miner is below the frozen ground, ore can be hoisted to the surface.

Some miners change history. At Franklin Gulch in 1887, Fred Hutchinson finds a way to mine all year instead of two months in the summer after the rock solid ground thaws. Essentially, fire thaws the ground to the point that dirt and gravel can be mined even in the winter. Mining is never the same after that. Productivity increases 500%.

Simple things bring joy to the early settlers, such as a window made out of a dozen or more white ginger-ale bottles, set vertically in the opening the thickness of a log that lets muted light inside a 10 x 14 foot cabin.

The miners cope with ruthless cold snaps, burn bacon grease for light, accurately calculate temperature even after the mercury thermometer freezes at about –40° F, shrewdly assess the amount of gold in a hill, sluice, build cabins, cut wood, cook, launder, cut hair, and open new claims.

They hunt game to live and do not waste anything. It would not surprise them that one of the Quest rules states that if a musher kills a game animal in defense of life or property, the racer must gut the animal and make arrangements for further salvage of the meat. It is the northern way.

Natural justice

The settlers don't like government but insist on natural justice. Murder, suicide, theft, and con games are frequent. Justice is uneven. Everybody is in the same boat.

Soapy Smith ruled Skagway for almost a year before the community rallied and drove his gang out of town. Fred Reid sacrificed his life in confronting Smith.

The criminal has few places to hide, and northern justice when activated is swift with no appeals. In contrast, if a miner hands his sack of gold to a saloon keeper, he puts it in an unlocked

115

drawer that is safer than a bank in Seattle.

When crime gets out of hand, brave citizens band together. In 1898, Soapy Smith, a personable, but nasty con man, and his gang rule Skagway for almost a year with an iron fist, softened by Robin Hood touches. Soapy sets money aside to take in abandoned dogs.

Frank Reid leads the vigilantes to challenge the con man. He kills Smith and Smith kills him. But the vigilantes succeed in banishing thieves, crooked gamblers, and con men. Natural justice carves out a sense of community.

Valued for who you are

The community values people for their energy, vigor, and courage, not by their position in society or their pretensions. People can be anonymous and private in the north. The community neither demands nor expects to know a person's background and credentials. Action in the now dominates what used to be.

Rich and poor share beer and stories. People help each other because they want to. They know that they can be on the receiving end of help in a blink of an eye. They leave their houses unlocked, especially in isolated regions, because it is a potential haven in an emergency.

Today's communities

The stories of the north, profoundly deep and forged in the cauldron of survival, ambition, tenacity, and the surreal reinforce the northern identity. History hovers closer to the surface here.

Stories about black bears and grizzly bears, moose, and wolves, men, women, and dogs of the gold rush, mushing and dog sled racing, First Nations natives, mining, claim jumping and geological reports glue the collective consciousness together in a dazzling, chaotic, narrative mix.

Authors like Jack London, Robert Service, and Pierre Berton receive public acclaim, but the oral tradition thrives wherever people gather. Day-to-day activities become first reports. A few survive as memorable reports, and, if dramatic enough, become repeated stories. They are the great anecdotes, bigger than life adventures, or allegories.

They rejuvenate the collective consciousness of the north that reflects who the northerner is.

Anne Tayler is a teacher, story teller, business woman, and Frank's partner.

Frank's partner, Anne, energetically promotes story telling. She creates, along with Louise Profeit-LeBlanc in 1988, the Yukon International Storytelling Festival, which Whitehorse hosts annually.

Storytellers join Yukon native elders to tell and sing stories in 30 different languages. Performers come from every part of the world. They sing, dance, mime, dramatize, and above all, tell stories.

Anne understands that the history, imagination, and vision in narratives create a community and hold it together more than wooden structures and isolated clumps of people.

When a man or woman, young or old, tells a story, the person becomes a narrator who passes on moral preferences, hope, survival skills, warnings, pragmatic advice, and essentially a gift that orally cascades down generations like living spirits.

People still remember a grandfather who joined the gold rush. Relatives are not too far from the first stampeders climbing Chilkoot Pass.

Supplies, information, legalities, and social interaction center in towns, but the community spreads across the whole region linked by supply lines, point-to-point pockets of people, a few roads, and above all stories.

Alaska covers 571,951 square miles, about four times larger than California. It has a population of 649,000 people, over 50 times smaller than California. The density averages about one person per square mile and one house per two square miles.

The Yukon is even less dense than Alaska with about 29,000 people living in 170,895 square miles, about one person per ten square miles.

However, two-way radio, satellite dishes, Internet, helicopters, snowmobiles, and bush planes link the whole region like one gigantic series of town hall meetings. The sense of community is more cohesive over the spread out wilderness than an anonymous neighborhood in a big city.

Iconic support

The communities support anybody idiosyncratic enough, northern enough to touch their lives. The mushers and their dogs fill the bill. The Yukon Quest represents everything the northerners love.

The mushers defy isolation by linking the most remote pockets of people even in serious conditions. They take on the sensuous mistress of the north sharing her beauty, some say with too many, and withstanding her cruelty. The mushers are living stories and reminders of the near past.

The whole northern community celebrates the Quest. The string of tiny towns, both on the U.S. and Canadian side, supports the mushers and dogs, veterinarians, officials, volunteers, family and friends who contribute to the Quest.

The communities refuse to let the musher pay for food or drink or accommodation. In 1987, an enterprising "outsider" at Biederman's Cabin violates an unspoken rule. He charges the mushers for food and room. The soup costs $5 and a room costs $40. The community ignores him. Not long after, he moves back to the city where they appreciate capitalism.

Strings of towns

Braeburn Lodge, the first checkpoint out of Whitehorse, welcomes the mushers with legendarily large food. The cinnamon bun weighs so much that the musher has to leave half his supplies behind to compensate.

By the time the dogs reach Carmacks, they travel 187 miles. During a two-hour mandatory layover, the vets check the dogs. This leg weeds out the unsound dogs. The officials check with the mushers to see whether the Quest is playing out as expected.

At McCabe Creek, the Kruse family serves warm drinks and big tubs of moose barley soup, and provides a warm shack for mushers all heated by solar or diesel power.

At Pelly Crossing the fire alarm bells ring for ten minutes to let people know when Frank arrives. The First Nations pull at Frank. Frank began his career in sociology working with the First Nations.

Now the elders tell him that they pray for him. He feels special, privileged to have the blessing of the First Nation elders, not is it an honor, but it motivates. Many elders remember when they drove dogs fifty years earlier along the same trails.

At the height of the gold rush, money buys anything and most anybody. Merchants sell the finest Parisian fashions and the best champagne. Showmen, merchants, bar owners, and madams work the streets of Dawson, not the creeks along the rivers. Dawson survives on tourism today.

A thousand miles from nowhere, Quest volunteers transform Scroggie Creek, which only has a 16 square meter cabin, into a musher's camp reminiscent of a Hollywood set with sleeping tents and shelters for the dogs, vets and officials. The make over blitz is the Yukon version of home renovation.

Eagle, Alaska, welcomes the competitors at any hour with a roaring bonfire. The Quest marks their winter festival.

Circle, Alaska, treats each musher like a movie star with brightly colored, customized banners decorated by the children. The town has one saloon. It used to have 28.

Cassiar Creek, where the 40-Mile and Yukon Rivers meet, lures the mushers with more food, a stop-the-world stew made by Shelly and Sabastien.

At Crabb's Corners in Central, the Quest volunteers craft a pro-totype dog lot with mushers' supplies, hot water, fuel, excellent food, and hearty hospitality. Also, a laundromat is available.

The spirit of the north hospitality not only looks after the mushers at tiny and remote places like Stepping Stone, Trout Creek, Biederman's, Slaven's, Dill's and Cochrane's Cabins, but they welcome any other traveler coming down the river.

Veterinarians, volunteers, and officials

The Whitehorse to Fairbanks route is a stage for many players who have their exits and their entrances. The plot is not as complicated as Shakespeare's *As You Like It*, but the characters and activity are as frantic and colorful.

Professional communities overlap informal communities. Veterinarians, volunteers, and officials bump into and help each other. The mushers work closely with the veterinarians throughout the year, including the International Sled Dog Veterinary Medical Association (ISDVMA).

Eleven veterinarians, from around the world, who focus their skills on racing sled dogs, work the trails at ten checkpoints to make sure the dogs have the appropriate weight, have feet that are in good condition, and are sufficiently hydrated and fed. Critically, the dogs must show that they are willing to run.

The roles in the Quest interlock and complement each other. It is a tribal community with its authority (International Council, International Boards), rule keepers (Rules Committee, Race Manager, Checkpoint and Dog Drop Managers, Race Marshal and Judges), support systems (Head Veterinarian and support veterinarians, volunteers, community members, and media) and competitors (mushers and dogs).

I love the language of the Quest objectives. First, it allows any **fit and experienced competitor** to participate in an epic. They understand that the toughest dog sled race in the world is a bigger than life drama with emergent plots and subplots, psychological games, and physical tests. They put the Quest in the league of Homer's *Iliad*.

Second, the Quest recognizes and promotes the **spirit that compels one to live in the Great North Land**. They understand the ineffable aesthetics that don't simply attract, but irresistibly pull people to the north. They like the fact that the international spirit cannot be controlled by political boundaries. They want attention focused on the historic development of people and animals.

Third, the Quest commemorates **human's dependence on sled dogs**. They see the dogs as the best friends of men and women. Conversely, they want to be the dogs' best friends.

Fourth, the Quest encourages and facilitates knowledge and application of the widest variety of **bush skills and practices** that form the foundation of Arctic survival.

The objective harkens back to the original settlers who survive by their wits. The musher and his dogs travel long isolated stretches in unpredictable weather. In a catastrophe, help is often days away.

Fifth, the Quest offers an experience that reflects the **spirit and perseverance of the pioneers** who discovered themselves in their wild search for adventure, glory, and wealth in the frozen north.

They know that no matter what happens, the mushers will learn something, especially about themselves, in their quest. Wealth may not be as abundant in the hills and creeks, but it is plentiful in the northerners themselves.

No whips

Finally, I point to a controversial, and particularly telling rule that forbids the use of whips, but reflects the third objective. This position stands in sharp contrast to Jim Welch's position in *The Speed Mushing Manual* (1989).

He maintains that the whip is an effective tool to generate a startle response that triggers an escape reflex in the dog, to punish a dog in extreme situations, and to condition the dog to avoid a certain behavior by not being disciplined. Welch says, "The whip hurts the dog but does not injure him."

The Quest says, "You don't get to hurt the dogs."

Frank's support

Frank receives international community support from as far away as Japan, Australia, New Zealand, and Europe. He receives support from both the northern community and the Yukon.

Above all, he receives support from what began as a small dog business, but is now transformed into a community that touches young lives, international visitors, and his own extended family. He creates a community and the community, in turn, gives him what he desires most—reassurance.

Many people play their parts, some in formal support, and others in background support. Each contribution hails the courage and skill of yesterday's and today's mushers and dogs. The tribute binds and reminds northerners of who they are and where they have come from. They see themselves in the Quest teams.

The Quest cannot exist without the spirit of community that grounds itself in values derived from brave, dreaming, tolerant traders, trappers, and miners tempered by both harshness and beauty of the land, tempered by romance and mystical balanced with the pragmatic.

Northern support

Mushers and their dogs race across a wondrous mountainous backdrop in frigid and isolated conditions. Notably they race from community to community, some so isolated that there are just three ways to get to them: dogsled, bush plane, or birth.

They warmly welcome the traveler with hearty and sincere hospitality. At the same time, various groups, including veterinarians, dog handlers, volunteers, and media, parallel the mushers' movements to support them.

Even when the musher is the only person on the trail hundreds of miles from nowhere, the community spirits surround, support, and sustain him.

The northern community celebrates the mushers. Each odyssey becomes their odyssey. Each Quest yields rich stories that inspire.

Task #6 for passionate leaders

Passionate leaders work with all kinds of communities. They understand the strength of people interacting with people, spirits touching spirits. They know how to create synergies with them.

The overlapping communities include extended families, networks of friends, formal organizations, and bigger social groups. They include knowledge keepers, masters of craft, professionals, and artists.

Connections generate connections

You find what you need in communities. Opportunities to learn abound. The six degrees of separation, often fewer, supposedly link everybody to everybody.

It is a fun exercise finding a chain to anybody and everybody. Often the connections seem tenuous, corny, and artificial. Nevertheless, four instances pop into my mind liking me to a musher, two Presidents, and a star entertainer.

Frank Turner at Muktuk Kennels knows Dick Gleason in Whitehorse, Yukon, who works with my uncle in 1980 in the Yukon.

George Bush knows Bob Brown who runs as Republican candidate for Governor for Montana in 2004 who debates with me on the team in 1970 at Montana State University.

Bette Midler grew up in the same neighborhood in New York as Cynthia whose Ph.D. dissertation I directed at Purdue University.

John Kennedy knew Marilyn Monroe whose husband, Arthur Miller, was visiting Professor in the Communication Department at the University of Michigan where I had my first teaching job.

The power of a friend who knows, commends, or refers a friend speeds the perception of trust and conviviality. *If Mary trusts her, then I can.*

Coincidence aside, one connection leads to other connections, like fractals repeating endlessly.

Leaders who craft communities of support excite the employees and their employees. The organization hums.

Small gestures of support often become symbolically big for the community. An owner of a 70 person welding company flies one of his employees to the Solomon Islands for his father's funeral.

The unsolicited support becomes part of the company folklore binding them together more than a wage increase. Applications to work for the company dramatically increase substantially.

In-house communities

The most immediate community work that passionate leaders do is with their own companies. They don't have to second-guess what employees see as support beyond monetary compensation. Just ask them.

Workers in a packaging company readily pinpoint three things. First, they want the work area painted. Second, they want windows for natural light in the work area. Third, they want a fund from which workers can easily get a short-term loan.

The employees design the color scheme. It costs $2400 to paint. The windows cost $14,000. The natural light softens the setting and brightens moods. The short-term loan fund costs are nominal. It is used 12 times in the year with no defaults.

Company support begins with asking. The question itself signals support. The timely responses also signal support. The gestures of support are small; the accumulated good will is large.

Great companies, however, go beyond what many employees imagine is possible. They help buy a home, redirect a career, or send them into the field to watch the consumers actually use the company's product.

Dog loyalty emerges when the individuals feel like a community, not because they wear the same uniform and come to the same building, but because they feel like a community. They identify with the company. They feel cohesive and convivial.

As citizens of the community, they feel responsibilities beyond a paycheck. A mother who sends her son to college, a couple who acquire their first home, and a young intern working on a special project with experienced staff do not whimsically forget the relationship.

External communities

Passionate leaders foster support from a variety of external communities including suppliers, media, regulators, rule makers, associations, competitors, consumers, researchers, teachers, and non-profit organizations.

When one of the previously mentioned companies faces extortion, 30 suppliers agree to accept a 100 day payment rather than the usual 30 days. In contrast, when a company in the same market faces a crisis, the same suppliers scramble to claim assets through the courts. The first company fosters the community of suppliers, the second company distains them.

Get working relationships with the media, regulators, and rule makers before your company ever gets close to a crisis situation. Once the crisis comes, mechanisms kick in that are hard to stop or change. A good relationship secures the best hearing.

Recognition

Recognition is the greatest support a leader can give a member of a community. It is a form of reassurance. It is the coin of the realm of any relationship. Recognition is life affirming. The action seems small but speaks loudly.

In contrast, when members of a community do not recognize a person, the person becomes invisible, perhaps ostracized or stigmatized, *persona non grata* (literally a person not accepted).

Lack of recognition makes people sick, disgruntled, angry, depressed, or vindictive. Recognition and reassurance are the glue of communities. Make sure you have it!

Meaningful, timely, non-gratuitous, honest, sincere recognition shows understanding, care, empathy, and love. Employees value random acts of kindness more than incremental gains from formal contracts.

Your quest happens in the context of multiple communities that judge your values and actions. The feedback that you receive either fuels the fire of success or dampens enthusiasm. Positive feedback energizes.

A quotation from George Bernard Shaw's *Man and Superman* highlights the connection between an individual and a community:

I am of the opinion that my life belongs to the whole community and as long as I live it is my privilege to do for it whatever I can. I want to be thoroughly used up when I die, for the harder I work, the more I live. I rejoice in life for it's own sake. Life is no "brief candle" to me. It is sort of a splendid torch which I have a hold of for the moment, and I want to make it burn as brightly as possible before handing it over to future generations. (George Bernard Shaw, *Man and Superman*, Epistle Dedicatory)

Your journey depends upon the macrocosms of interconnected people where the coin of the realm is recognition and reassurance.

Six tasks for passionate leaders

Being a passionate leader is fun. You wake up looking forward to each day. The chase is on. You know where you are going. Your values are right. You have the right people in the right jobs. You have permission to lead. Your will is made of iron. And, you give to the community.

The payoff is huge and satisfying. It is discovery, connection, learning, and self-knowledge.

The "call of the wild" is a call to unleash your passion as a leader. The source of the call is inside of you, not outside. Periodically, parts of the song quietly sing to you.

> . . . the call still sounding in the depths of the forest. It filled him with a great unrest and strange desires. It caused him to feel a vague, sweet gladness, and he was aware of wild yearnings and stirrings for he knew not what. (Jack London, *The call of the wild*)

Listen to its music. Hear its message. Explore the "wild yearnings and stirrings" of leadership. Get six tasks in place:

1. Get a worthy quest!
2. Bring life to your values!
3. Get the right people in the right jobs!
4. Obtain permission to lead!
5. Develop an iron will!
6. Foster community support!

Task #1: Get a worthy quest!

Worthy quests lurk within you like sleeping giants. You need to release one from its cage of sleep. When it awakens, it will have tremendous resolve.

The key to the awakening begins with answering simple questions, which, in essence, are just versions of the same question:

> *What do I want to do?*
>
> *If I could wave a magic wand and obtain something significant in my life, what would it be?*
>
> *How do I want to be remembered?*
>
> *If I won the lottery, what would I do with it?*
>
> *What have I not tried, but have always wanted to try?*
>
> *What am I afraid to try, but am drawn to?*

Dream! Imagine! Be brave! Every person needs a worthy quest, not just leaders of big corporations. A quest is an investment in yourself. Get one that suits you.

Get a quest that is ambitious and doable. It takes you out of your comfort zone, but it is possible. Above all, find a quest in which you will learn, one that takes you to new realms, understanding, and appreciation.

Don't endlessly look for the perfect quest. That is procrastination. There are many worthy quests. If you can't decide from a half dozen quests that appeal to you, then choose one randomly. The Muses will be kind.

Don't let the magnitude of the quest paralyze you. The 1000-mile journey begins with one step outside your door, then another, and another. Break the quest into parts within your capabilities. Work incrementally from goal to goal until you reach the largest goal.

You cannot fail with a worthy quest. You inevitably learn. If you are wildly successful, you touch and teach others, contribute to various communities, and gain deeper knowledge. Worthy quests are addictive. As one quest leads to another, fantastic journeys fill your life. The call of the wild no longer lurks in the background; it has burst into full song.

Task #2: Bring life to your values!

Dylan Thomas writes in a plea to his dying father, *"Do not go gentle into that good night, Old age should burn and rave at close of day. Rage, rage against the dying light."*

But, don't wait until you are close to your last breath to burn and rave and rage. Let people see the values of your life now. Let your values rage. Be courageous.

Do not go gentle into this good life. Create white water. Let your values tumble down the rapids touching lives. When you bring life to your values, your **certainty becomes a strength.**

Ronald Reagan's unambiguous, optimistic perspective stood in sharp contrast to the malaise that Jimmy Carter portrayed. Americans don't know what a malaise is. George W. Bush's positions on Iraq, gay marriages, and religion stood in sharp contrast to John Kerry's complex and qualified positions that rambled over the countryside. People do not like to guess where their leaders stand.

Certainty creates more energy. Difficult choices do not paralyze you. Indecision does not stop you. You react quickly with confidence. Your focus is sharper.

Consequently, you feel full of life, vigorous, and active. Others see your actions grounded in values which you live not merely proclaim. They see your daily values rather than the dusty set hauled out in crisis. They see your authentic values rather than a contrived version spin-doctored by a public relations consultant.

People see you as more sincere and trustworthy because you freely and demonstrably embrace your values, not because you have to, but because you want to.

135

have to, but because you want to.

When you bring life to your values, you take a stand. You do not hide behind the passive: *Whatever happens, happens*. You do not retreat to the apparent safety of the neutral: *I'm neither for nor against it*. You do not mask your insecurity with the negative: *She could have done better. It is not the worst thing he did*.

Can you imagine Jesus Christ, Martin Luther King, or Mohammed, being carefully passive, strategically neutral, or sarcastically negative?

Rage, rage against a nondescript, grey, uncommitted life. Bring life to your values!

Task #3: Get the right people in the right jobs!

Part of the fun of *Mission Impossible*, a late 1960's espionage show, is mentally helping the team leader who sorts through a repertoire of people who have different skills. He has to create an ideal team—get the right people for the right job—to accomplish the unfeasible assignment.

Although *Mission Impossible* would have you believe that a disguise artist, an electronics technician, a strong man, and a seductress can solve any world crisis, the exercise of imagining the right team is useful. It is something you should do for yourself.

Namely, you should find ideal teams for your personal life and work life. The task begins with declaring what you care about, deciding what you want or need to do, and understanding what the "right jobs" are. *Do you care about personal growth? Do you want to increase efficiency, sales, or productivity? Do you need to maximize team performance? Do you yearn for better creativity?*

Once you decide the right jobs, then finding the right people follows. A world of expertise waits for you. Seek strong, energetic, and interesting individuals. Find experienced, smart, and wise people. They invigorate and challenge. They make you more robust, resilient, and tolerant.

Do not choose people who drain energy, undermine confidence, or belittle. Do not accept inappropriate people who happen to be there because of coincidence, convenience, or proximity. The wrong person in the wrong job squanders opportunities through indifference, inefficiency, sloppy work, sabotage, waste, apathy, abuse, laziness, or a myriad of other behaviors.

Once you accept people for a job, they, in turn, will influence, shape, and affect your life. They will change you. The right people create synergy. They perform beyond expectations. Job parameters appropriately expand, and efficiency increases.

The task of getting the right people for the right job is so important that you must be the custodian of getting the optimal match. Then, the accountability rests where it belongs, and you have a great chance of running a 1000-mile race with a high performing team.

Task #4: Obtain permission to lead!

If you make it this far in the book, you have tacitly given me permission to lead you for a short period through a series of associations triggered by a special man in the Yukon. Thank you for consenting to the journey.

As important as all the other tasks are, this task entails the most powerful lesson—namely, **passionate leaders obtain permission to lead.** My friend, Euan, likes to say that he works with ordinary people who do extraordinary things, and they do. It is because they give him permission to lead.

The good mushers talk to their dogs, not merely to drive and command them, but to get permission. As a passionate leader, talk to individuals intimately and sincerely. People desire this type of interaction. Have authentic and genuine conversations with them. People crave it, especially in a world driven by spin, political correctness, and alarmist rhetoric.

Ask them rather than tell them. Consult them rather than disconfirm them. Recognize them rather than ignore them. Nothing shows more respect than this type of talk. Nothing has more potential to motivate individuals than respectful communication.

When you ask, consult, and recognize, you empower individuals. The permission that they have to grant now can powerfully validate and legitimize the relationship. When they give you permission to lead, they enter a tacit contract to be part of the solution, an active agent, and a partner in the endeavor.

At this point, the genie is out of the bottle. The granted permission liberates the magic and power of a "relationship" which is free and unconstrained to create, perform, and deliver.

Task #5: Develop an iron will!

Would you develop an iron will for $10 million dollars? If you say, "*Yes, I would,*" then the money is irrelevant really. So, what is stopping you now, the lack of offer?

Developing an iron will is a paradoxical process because you are both the "will maker" and "will taker." "*I will do it*" entails a creator-like activity, going from nothing to something.

It seems like an impossible trick, like the big bang creation of the universe, something from nothing. *How did that happen? Where did something come from to bang in the first place?* Once the universe explodes into existence, it expands indeterminably. Once your will explodes with "*I will do it,*" it too can expand indeterminably.

I like stories about Lance Armstrong overcoming cancer and winning, William Kleedehn struggling up Eagle Summit in the Yukon Quest, the 9/11 heroes, and the stampeders climbing Chilkoot.

Each story whispers to my "will maker" to be a better person, give more, work harder, be more tolerant, get healthier, and learn more. You can't do anything or everything, but you can do many things when you will it. Now, the challenge, and amazing mental trick, is to want to do it!

Task #6: Foster community support!

Philip Nolan in Everett Hale's *Man without a country* is a dead soul. Without a community, there is no meaning in his life. Without a community, he has no identity. He goes to his grave never being able to simply say, "*This is my own, my native land.*"

A passionate leader finds meaning, identity, and solace in the community. A large and diverse community presents countless opportunities to find resources, discover talent, learn new information, and be repeatedly surprised and pleased. It offers the greatest opportunity for synergy.

The community offers more than supplies and services. People connected to people anchor one another. They shape each other's values, beliefs, and personalities. Individuals, taken together, as a community, determine convention, mores, education, and laws, and they are a significant source of recognition and affirmation.

The passionate leader participates in and gives back to the community, not out of obligation, but because it brings the satisfaction of knowing, "*This is my own . . . .*" Fostering community support helps you answer the call of the wild.

140

Beginning

Passionate leadership is full of fire. It is hot, active, and burning. It changes and transforms. A chain reaction of events occurs when you get the six tasks in place.

When you get a worthy goal, you become **purposeful** and embrace intent.

When you bring life to your values, you speak and act with courage. The **conviction of certainty** centers your actions.

When you get the right people in the right jobs, you accept the **responsibility and accountability** of making things happen.

When you obtain permission to lead, you **humbly develop relationships** that respect and recognize people. The contract tacitly connects an authentic "you" to other individuals.

When you develop an iron will, you demonstrate **resolve**. You are steadfast, tenacious, and dogged.

When you foster community support, you find **meaning** and embrace an identity. You move from the subjective to the objective. You allow yourself to be affirmed and recognised by others.

At the beginning of this book, I invited you to take a journey with me, make connections to your life, relationships, and work, and listen to the call of the wild stirring within you. The extended metaphor of treating people like dogs, leads to six life tasks that every passionate leader should have. Today is a good day to continue the journey.

Annotated references

Adney, Tappan. *The Klondike stampede*. Vancouver: Harper & Brothers Publishers. 1900. As a special correspondent of *Harper's Weekly*, Adney brings a reporter's eye to the Yukon history.

Balzar, John. *Yukon alone: The world's toughest adventure race*. New York, New York: Henry Holt and Company. 1999. His prose is personal, energetic, and wonderfully idiosyncratic.

Block, Peter. *Flawless consulting: A guide to getting your expertise used*. San Francisco: Jossey-Bass/Pfeiffer. 1981. And, *Stewardship*. San Francisco: Berrett-Koehler Publishers. 1993. Peter's work changed my perception of leadership. His influence indirectly took me to Muktuk.

Cervantes Saavedra, Miguel de. *Don Quixote*. Translated by Edith Grossman. New York: Harper Collins Publishers, 2003. He understood the quest as a quest.

Cohen, Stan. *The streets were paved with gold: A pictorial history of the Klondike gold rush 1896-1899*. Missoula, Montana: Pictorial Histories Publishing Co. 1977. Stan is an extraordinary archivist and historical author focusing on the visual. His photographic collection is remarkable.

Darling, Esther Birdsall. *Baldy of Nome*. Philadelphia: The Penn Publishing Co. 1924.

Firth, John. *Yukon Quest: The 1,000-mile dog sled race through the Yukon and Alaska*. Lost Moose: Whitehorse, Yukon. 1998. Firth's book comprehensively covers the Quest from 1984 when it began to 1997. He has a delightful style for writing and he is one of the local experts.

IKEA. www.ikea.com. IKEA is consistently on "Best Companies to Work for" lists.

International Sled Dog Veterinary Medical Association (ISDVMA). This association is the best source for solid research on the dogs involved with dog sledding. Dr. Kathleen McGill, Head Veterinarian for 2005 Yukon Quest, was extremely helpful in discussing the research on dogs. Also, Dr. Jerry Vanek was very generous with his time. He has served as a Chief Veterinarian or Trail Veterinarian at over 50 sled dog races, more than any other veterinarian in the world. His practical and theoretical knowledge of these dogs brings joy. He graciously and gently guided me with a careful read of this book.

Killick, Adam. *Racing the white silence: On the trail of the Yukon Quest.* Person, Canada: Penguin Canada. 2002. Adam is an award-winning writer, photographer, and a dog handler for Frank Turner in 2002.

London, Jack. *The call of the wild.* New York, New York: S. S. McClure Company. 1905. *The Saturday Evening Post* serialized the story June 20-July 18, 1903. And, *To build a fire.* New York, New York: S. S. McClure Company. 1905. First published in *The Century Magazine*, v.76, August, 1908, 525-534. See also *The white silence and other tales of the north, White Fang, and Brown Wolf.*

Muir, John. *Stickeen.* Afterword by Malcolm Margolin. Berkeley: Heyday Books. 1981. John took over a decade to craft the story of Stickeen which is told in a half dozen books. Stickeen's story can be found on www.yosemite.ca.us/john_muir_writings/stickeen.

Murphy, Claire Rudolf and **Haigh, Jane G**. *Gold rush dogs.* Alaska Northwest Books. Anchorage, Portland, 2001. Jane graciously helped us locate the pictures of Balto, Baldy, and Julian in this book. She also put us in touch with Bill Berry.

Satterfield, Archie. *Chilkoot Pass*. Alaska Northwest Books. Portland, Oregon, 2004. Satterfield gives an account of the stampede to the Klondike goldfields and an authoritative guide for hiking over the pass.

Thomas, Dylan. *The Poems of Dylan Thomas*. New Directions, 1952. Dylan probably composed the poem in 1945 when his father was dying.

Welch, Jim. *The speed mushing manual: How to train racing sled dogs*. Eagle River, Alaska: Sirius Publishing. 1989. Today, Jim says that the debate about whips is a non-issue. Breeds and training have changed. But, at the time his position was common. (Telephone conversation on August 17, 2005)

Yukon Historical & Museums Association. *The Kohklux Map*. This map and story is published in association with Klukwan Village Council, Council for Yukon Indians, Yukon Archives and Aboriginal Language Services. Whitehorse, Yukon, Canada, 1995.

Photo and illustrator credits

George Carmack, Tagish Charley, and Skookum Jim (p. 11). Sketch by Joe Boddy. Copyright Stan Cohen, Pictorial Histories Publishing Co., Missoula, Montana.

Excelsior docking at San Francisco (p. 12). University of Washington Libraries, Special Collections, UW 14504.

Chilkoot Pass (p. 14). University of Washington Libraries, Special Collections, Hegg 97.

Chilkoot Pass viewed from top (p. 15). University of Washington Libraries, Special Collections, Hegg 98.

Maps. Whitehorse to Dawson (p. 18), Dawson to Eagle Summit (p. 19), and Eagle Summit to Fairbanks (p. 20). Illustrated by Robert Norton in collaboration with Frank Turner, wildnortonfire@ecn.net.au.

Muktuk photos. Buck (p. 43), Frank and three dogs (Color plate 1), Puppies (Color plate 4), Pre-race 2005 at Whitehorse (Color plate 9), Race start 2005 at Whitehorse (Color plate 10), Frank's dogs in tent at Dawson (Color plate 13), Frank on river (Color plate 14), Anne Tayler (Color 16), Dogs at play (Color plate 17), 2005 Quest dogs (Color plates 18 through 31), Anne Tayler at festival (p. 117), Frank with dog (front cover), Frank with dogs on curve (back cover).

Robert Norton photos. Muktuk Kennels (Color plate 2), Heidi, Marie, and Rob (Color plate 3), Dinner at Muktuk (Color plate 5), and Mural at MacBride Museum (Color plate 7), wildnortonfire@ecn.net.au.

146

White Horse Rapids **mural** (Color plate 7). Original artwork by Edith Jerome, Whitehorse, Yukon. It took about one year to paint the mural on the side of the MacBride Museum in Whitehorse.

Aurora Borealis (Color plate 6). Dick Hutchinson, Circle, Alaska. Dick photographed the northern lights for over two decades. He generously shares his knowledge of photographing the aurora on various websites. Hutchinson's photographs truly inspire. I deeply appreciate his contribution. Search for "aurora borealis" on Google.

Carsten Theis's photos. Frank at 2005 banquet (Color plate 8), Frank preparing straw (Color plate 11), Frank congratulating dogs at Dawson (Color plate 12), Frank on way to Dawson (Color plate 15), and William Kleedehn at Eagle Summit (p. 95). Carsten has been exceptionally helpful with these photographs. He has a great eye for the dramatic. Carsten lives in Fairbanks, Alaska.

Stickeen (p. 61). Illustrated by Carl Buell. Heyday Publications owns the copyright.

Working dogs (p. 62). Tappen Adney photographed the dogs. The University of British Columbia owns the copyright.

Julian (p. 67). Courtesy of William F. Berry. He wrote a delightful letter to me recounting the exploits of Julian and his ancestors. He lives in Alaska. His grandfather worked with Julian.

Baldy (p. 83). The photo is from *Baldy of Nome* (1924) by Ester Birdsall Darling.

Balto and Gunner (p. 88). Cleveland Public Library, Photographic Collection.

Drift mining (p. 114). Illustrated by Robert Norton using old sketches of this type of mining, wildnortonfire@ecn.net.au.

147

Soapy Smith (p. 115). Alaska State Library (ASL) Early Prints of Alaska Collection (01-1976), Juneau, Alaska.

Index

Call of the Wild

Workshops in the Yukon for Passionate Leaders

Call of the Wild workshops take you on a mythic and epic journey to explore six tasks that passionate leaders must get in place. Productivity increases, energy jumps, spirits soar, and creativity explodes when this happens. The workshop includes an optional camping trip and a visit to Muktuk Kennels to meet Frank Turner, veteran Yukon Quest musher, and his northern dogs who are super athletes.

Who should attend? Executives, senior managers, and teams who want to foster passionate leadership.

Time and location: We offer workshops throughout the year. Whitehorse, capital of the Yukon Territory provides a setting that suits the journey for renewal, rejuvenation, and discovery. Check website for other locations.

Details: Telephone Robert Norton at 310 413 4050 or register online at www.wildnortonfire.com. For other enquiries, email wildnortonfire@ecn.net.au.

About the author

Dr. Robert Norton specializes in change and intervention. He is an expert in crisis management, marketing, and executive coaching. He is an outstanding speaker.

Robert is a Fulbright Scholar who helped Australia in its AIDS Education and Prevention Programs (1988) in hospitals, school systems, clinics, businesses, and prisons.

He earned his B.A. at the Montana State University, his M.A. at the University of New Mexico, and his Ph.D. at the University of Wisconsin. As a researcher and scholar, he has written two books and over 35 professional journal articles and book chapters. As a Professor and teacher, he has over 22 years experience teaching at the graduate level in 12 universities. In 1994 he moved exclusively to private industry.

Robert is Director of Wild Norton Fire in the United States. He also is the Director of the Norton Consulting Group in Australia.

Contact Robert at wildnortonfire@ecn.net.au or telephone him at 310 413 4050.

Endorsement of *Treat People Like Dogs! Six Tasks for Passionate Leaders*

Corporate executives, middle managers, and scout troop leaders who read this book will discover what accomplished dog mushers have known for decades — "You can't push a rope!"

Author Robert Norton is the first management scholar to recognize and describe the fundamental leadership skills developed over the ages by mushers faced with the challenge of motivating their dog teams from behind using an essentially foreign language while in the most hostile of climates.

*Norton translates these leadership concepts into an easily understood, highly readable text for leaders and leaders-in-training across all strata of management. **This book is a must read for any leader contemplating their ultimate Quest.***

Dr. Jerry Vanek
Musher, Veterinarian, Researcher

Dr. Jerry Vanek is a charter board member of the International Sled Dog Veterinary Medical Association (ISDVMA). He has participated in research on sled dog diarrhea and cardiac enzymes and studied physical therapy for dogs at the Animal Rehabilitation Institute. Dr. Vanek served as a Chief Veterinarian or Trail Veterinarian at over 50 sled dog races, more than any other veterinarian in the world.